The Poems of Giacomo Leopardi

Giacomo Leopardi

Translated by Frederick Townsend

DODO
PRESS

THE POEMS OF GIACOMO LEOPARDI

TRANSLATED BY
FREDERICK TOWNSEND

1887

TO M. N. M.
SISTER OF THE TRANSLATOR
THESE POEMS
ARE AFFECTIONATELY INSCRIBED
BY
THE EDITOR

PREFACE.

Giacomo Leopardi is a great name in Italy among philosophers and poets, but is quite unknown in this country, and Mr. Townsend has the honor of introducing him, in the most captivating way, to his countrymen. In Germany and France he has excited attention. Translations have been made of his works; essays have been written on his ideas. But in England his name is all but unheard of. Six or seven years ago Mr. Charles Edwards published a translation of the essays and dialogues, but no version of the poems has appeared, so far as I know. Leopardi was substantially a poet, —that is to say, he had imagination, sentiment, passion, an intense love of beauty, a powerful impulse towards things ideal. The sad tone of his speculations about the universe and human destiny gave an impression of mournfulness to his lines, but this rather deepened the pathos of his work. In the same breath he sang of love and the grave, and the love was the more eager for its brevity. He had the poetic temperament—sensitive, ardent, aspiring. He possessed the poetic aspect—the broad white brow, the large blue eyes. Some compared him to Byron, but the resemblance was external merely. In ideas, purpose, feeling, he was entirely unlike the Englishman; in the energy and fire of his style only did he somewhat resemble him. Worshippers have even ventured to class him with Dante, a comparison which shows, at least, in what estimation the poet could be held at home, and how largely the patriotic sentiment entered into the conception of poetical compositions, how necessary it was that the singer should be a bard. His verses ranged over a large field. They were philosophic, patriotic, amorous. There are odes, lyrics, satires, songs; many very beautiful and feeling; all noble and earnest. His three poems, "All' Italia, " "Sopra il Monumento di Dante, " "A Angelo Mai, " gave him a national reputation. They touch the chords to which he always responded—patriotism, poetry, learning, a national idealism bearing aloft an enormous weight of erudition and thought.

Leopardi was born at Recanati, a small town about fifteen miles from Ancona, in 1798. He was of noble parentage, though not rich. His early disposition was joyous, but with the feverish joy of a highly-strung, nervous organization. He was a great student from boyhood; and severe application undermined a system that was never robust, and that soon became hopelessly diseased. Illness, accompanied with sharp pain, clipped the wings of his ambition, obliged him to forego preferment, and deepened the hopelessness that hung over his expectations. His hunger for love could not be satisfied, for his physical infirmity rendered a union undesirable, even if possible, while a craving ideality soon transcended any visible object of affection. He had warm friends of his own sex, one of whom, Antonio Ranieri, stayed by him in all vicissitudes, took him to Naples, and closed his eyes, June 14, 1837.

To this acute sensibility of frame must be added the torture of the heart arising from a difference with his father, who, as a Catholic, was disturbed by the skeptical tendencies of his son, and the perpetual irritation of a conflict with the large majority of even philosophical minds. An early death might have been anticipated. No amount of hopefulness, of zest for life, of thirst for opportunity, of genius for intellectual productiveness will counteract such predisposition to decay. The death of the body, however, has but ensured a speedier immortality of the soul; for many a thinker has since been busy in gathering up the fragments of his mind and keeping his memory fresh. His immense learning has been forgotten. His archaeological knowledge, which fascinated Niebuhr, is of small account to-day. But his speculative and poetical genius is a permanent illumination.

Mr. Townsend, the translator, well known in New York, where he was born, lived ten years in Italy, and seven in Rome. He was a studious, thoughtful man; quiet, secluded, scholarly; an eminent student of Italian literature; a real sympathizer with Italian progress. By the cast of his mind and the course of his inward experience he was drawn towards Leopardi. His version adheres as closely to the original as is compatible with elegance and the preservation of metrical grace. He has not rendered into English all Leopardi's poems, but he has presented the best of them, enough to give an idea of his author's style of feeling and expression. What he has done, has been performed faithfully. It is worth remarking that he was attracted by the intense longing of the poet for love and appreciation, and by keen sympathy with his unhappy condition. It is needless to say that he did not share the pessimism that imparts a melancholy hue to the philosopher's own doctrine, and that might have been modified if not dispelled by a different experience. The translation was finished at Siena, the summer of the earthquake, and was the last work Mr. Townsend ever did, the commotion outside not interrupting him, or causing him to suspend his application.

O. B. Frothingham.

CONTENTS.

Dedication.

[From the first Florentine Edition of the Poems, in the year 1831.]

To my Friends in Tuscany:

My dear Friends, I dedicate this book to you, in which, as is oft the case with Poets, I have sought to illustrate my sorrow, and with which I now—I cannot say it without tears—take leave of Literature and of my studies. I hoped these dear studies would have been the consolation of my old age, and thought, after having lost all the other joys and blessings of childhood and of youth, I had secured *one,* of which no power, no unhappiness could rob me. But I was scarcely twenty years old, when that weakness of nerves and of stomach, which has destroyed my life, and yet gives me no hope of death, robbed that only blessing of more than half its value, and, in my twenty-eighth year, has utterly deprived me of it, and, as I *must* think, forever. I have not been able to read these pages, and have been compelled to entrust their revision to other eyes and other hands. I will utter no more complaints, my dear friends; the consciousness of the depth of my affliction admits not of complaints and lamentations. I have lost all; I am a withered branch, that feels and suffers still. *You* only have I won! Your society, which must compensate me for all my studies, joys, and hopes, would almost outweigh my sorrows, did not my very sickness prevent me from enjoying it as I could wish, and did I not know that Fate will soon deprive me of this benefit, also, and will compel me to spend the remainder of my days, far from all the delights of civilized life, in a spot, far better suited to the dead than to the living. Your love, meanwhile, will ever follow me, and will yet cling to me, perhaps, when this body, which, indeed, no longer lives, shall be turned to ashes. Farewell! Your

Leopardi

TO ITALY. (1818.)

My country, I the walls, the arches see,
The columns, statues, and the towers
Deserted, of our ancestors;
But, ah, the glory I do not behold,
The laurel and the sword, that graced
Our sires of old.
Now, all unarmed, a naked brow,
A naked breast dost thou display.
Ah, me, how many wounds, what stains of blood!
Oh, what a sight art thou,
Most beautiful of women! I
To heaven cry aloud, and to the world:
"Who hath reduced her to this pass?
Say, say!" And worst of all, alas,
See, both her arms in chains are bound!
With hair dishevelled, and without a veil
She sits, disconsolate, upon the ground,
And hides her face between her knees,
As she bewails her miseries.
Oh, weep, my Italy, for thou hast cause;
Thou, who wast born the nations to subdue,
As victor, and as victim, too!
Oh, if thy eyes two living fountains were,
The volume of their tears could ne'er express
Thy utter helplessness, thy shame;
Thou, who wast once the haughty dame,
And, now, the wretched slave.
Who speaks, or writes of thee,
That must not bitterly exclaim:
"She once was great, but, oh, behold her now"?
Why hast thou fallen thus, oh, why?
Where is the ancient force?
Where are the arms, the valor, constancy?
Who hath deprived thee of thy sword?
What treachery, what skill, what labor vast,
Or what o'erwhelming horde
Whose fierce, invading tide, thou could'st not stem,
Hath robbed thee of thy robe and diadem?
From such a height how couldst thou fall so low?
Will none defend thee? No?

No son of thine? For arms, for arms, I call;
Alone I'll fight for thee, alone will fall.
And from my blood, a votive offering,
May flames of fire in every bosom spring!
Where are thy sons? The sound of arms I hear,
Of chariots, of voices, and of drums;
From foreign lands it comes,
For which thy children fight.
Oh, hearken, hearken, Italy! I see,—
Or is it but a dream?—
A wavering of horse and foot,
And smoke, and dust, and flashing swords,
That like the lightning gleam.
Art thou not comforted? Dost turn away
Thy eyes, in horror, from the doubtful fray?
Ye gods, ye gods. Oh, can it be?
The youth of Italy
Their hireling swords for other lands have bared!
Oh, wretched he in war who falls,
Not for his native shores,
His loving wife and children dear,
But, fighting for another's gain,
And by another's foe is slain!
Nor can he say, as his last breath he draws,
"My mother-land, beloved, ah see,
The life thou gav'st, I render back to thee!"
Oh fortunate and dear and blessed,
The ancient days, when rushed to death the brave,
In crowds, their country's life to save!
And you, forever glorious,
Thessalian straits,
Where Persia, Fate itself, could not withstand
The fiery zeal of that devoted band!
Do not the trees, the rocks, the waves,
The mountains, to each passer-by,
With low and plaintive voice tell
The wondrous tale of those who fell,
Heroes invincible who gave
Their lives, their Greece to save?
Then cowardly as fierce,
Xerxes across the Hellespont retired,
A laughing-stock to all succeeding time;
And up Anthela's hill, where, e'en in death

The sacred Band immortal life obtained,
Simonides slow-climbing, thoughtfully,
Looked forth on sea and shore and sky.
And then, his cheeks with tears bedewed,
And heaving breast, and trembling foot, he stood,
His lyre in hand and sang:
"O ye, forever blessed,
Who bared your breasts unto the foeman's lance,
For love of her, who gave you birth;
By Greece revered, and by the world admired,
What ardent love your youthful minds inspired,
To rush to arms, such perils dire to meet,
A fate so hard, with loving smiles to greet?
Her children, why so joyously,
Ran ye, that stern and rugged pass to guard?
As if unto a dance,
Or to some splendid feast,
Each one appeared to haste,
And not grim death Death to brave;
But Tartarus awaited ye,
And the cold Stygian wave;
Nor were your wives or children at your side,
When, on that rugged shore,
Without a kiss, without a tear, ye died.
But not without a fearful blow
To Persians dealt, and their undying shame.
As at a herd of bulls a lion glares,
Then, plunging in, upon the back
Of this one leaps, and with his claws
A passage all along his chine he tears,
And fiercely drives his teeth into his sides,
Such havoc Grecian wrath and valor made
Amongst the Persian ranks, dismayed.
Behold each prostrate rider and his steed;
Behold the chariots, and the fallen tents,
A tangled mass their flight impede;
And see, among the first to fly,
The tyrant, pale, and in disorder wild!
See, how the Grecian youths,
With blood barbaric dyed,
And dealing death on every side,
By slow degrees by their own wounds subdued,
The one upon the other fall. Farewell,

Ye heroes blessed, whose names shall live,
While tongue can speak, or pen your story tell!
Sooner the stars, torn from their spheres, shall hiss,
Extinguished in the bottom of the sea,
Than the dear memory, and love of you,
Shall suffer loss, or injury.
Your tomb an altar is; the mothers here
Shall come, unto their little ones to show
The lovely traces of your blood. Behold,
Ye blessed, myself upon the ground I throw,
And kiss these stones, these clods
Whose fame, unto the end of time,
Shall sacred be in every clime.
Oh, had I, too, been here with you,
And this dear earth had moistened with my blood!
But since stern Fate would not consent
That I for Greece my dying eyes should close,
In conflict with her foes,
Still may the gracious gods accept
The offering I bring,
And grant to me the precious boon,
Your Hymn of Praise to sing!"

ON DANTE'S MONUMENT, 1818.

(THEN UNFINISHED.)

Though all the nations now
Peace gathers under her white wings,
The minds of Italy will ne'er be free
From the restraints of their old lethargy,
Till our ill-fated land cling fast
Unto the glorious memories of the Past.
Oh, lay it to thy heart, my Italy,
Fit honor to thy dead to pay;
For, ah, their like walk not thy streets to-day!
Nor is there one whom thou canst reverence!
Turn, turn, my country, and behold
That noble band of heroes old,
And weep, and on thyself thy anger vent,
For without anger, grief is impotent:
Oh, turn, and rouse thyself for shame,
Blush at the thought of sires so great,
Of children so degenerate!

Alien in mien, in genius, and in speech,
The eager guest from far
Went searching through the Tuscan soil to find
Where he reposed, whose verse sublime
Might fitly rank with Homer's lofty rhyme;
And oh! to our disgrace he heard
Not only that, e'er since his dying day,
In other soil his bones in exile lay,
But not a stone within thy walls was reared
To him, O Florence, whose renown
Caused thee to be by all the world revered.
Thanks to the brave, the generous band,
Whose timely labor from our land
Will this sad, shameful stain remove!
A noble task is yours,
And every breast with kindred zeal hath fired,
That is by love of Italy inspired.

May love of Italy inspire you still,
Poor mother, sad and lone,

To whom no pity now
In any breast is shown,
Now, that to golden days the evil days succeed.
May pity still, ye children dear,
Your hearts unite, your labors crown,
And grief and anger at her cruel pain,
As on her cheeks and veil the hot tears rain!
But how can I, in speech or song,
Your praises fitly sing,
To whose mature and careful thought,
The work superb, in your proud task achieved,
Will fame immortal bring?
What notes of cheer can I now send to you,
That may unto your ardent souls appeal,
And add new fervor to your zeal?

Your lofty theme will inspiration give,
And its sharp thorns within your bosoms lodge.
Who can describe the whirlwind and the storm
Of your deep anger, and your deeper love?
Who can your wonder-stricken looks portray,
The lightning in your eyes that gleams?
What mortal tongue can such celestial themes
In language fit describe?
Away ye souls, profane, away!
What tears will o'er this marble stone be shed!
How can it fall? How fall your fame sublime,
A victim to the envious tooth of Time?
O ye, that can alleviate our woes,
Sole comfort of this wretched land,
Live ever, ye dear Arts divine,
Amid the ruins of our fallen state,
The glories of the past to celebrate!
I, too, who wish to pay
Due honor to our grieving mother, bring
Of song my humble offering,
As here I sit, and listen, where
Your chisel life unto the marble gives.
O thou, illustrious sire of Tuscan song,
If tidings e'er of earthly things,
Of *her*, whom thou hast placed so high,
Could reach your mansions in the sky,
I know, thou for thyself no joy wouldst feel,

For, with thy fame compared,
Renowned in every land,
Our bronze and marble are as wax and sand;
If thee we *have* forgotten, *can* forget,
May suffering still follow suffering,
And may thy race to all the world unknown,
In endless sorrows weep and moan.

Thou for thyself no joy wouldst feel,
But for thy native land,
If the example of their sires
Could in the cold and sluggish sons
Renew once more the ancient fires,
That they might lift their heads in pride again.
Alas, with what protracted sufferings
Thou seest her afflicted, that, e'en then
Did seem to know no end,
When thou anew didst unto Paradise ascend!
Reduced so low, that, as thou seest her now,
She then a happy Queen appeared.
Such misery her heart doth grieve,
As, seeing, thou canst not thy eyes believe.
And oh, the last, most bitter blow of all,
When on the ground, as she in anguish lay,
It seemed, indeed, thy country's dying day!

O happy thou, whom Fate did not condemn
To live amid such horrors; who
Italian wives didst not behold
By ruffian troops embraced;
Nor cities plundered, fields laid waste
By hostile spear, and foreign rage;
Nor works divine of genius borne away
In sad captivity, beyond the Alps,
The roads encumbered with the precious prey;
Nor foreign rulers' insolence and pride;
Nor didst insulting voices hear,
Amidst the sound of chains and whips,
The sacred name of Liberty deride.
Who suffers not? Oh! at these wretches' hands,
What have we not endured?
From what unholy deed have they refrained?
What temple, altar, have they not profaned?

Why have we fallen on such evil times?
Why didst thou give us birth, or why
No sooner suffer us to die,
O cruel Fate? We, who have seen
Our wretched country so betrayed,
The handmaid, slave of impious strangers made,
And of her ancient virtues all bereft;
Yet could no aid or comfort give.
Or ray of hope, that might relieve
The anguish of her soul.
Alas, my blood has not been shed for thee,
My country dear! Nor have I died
That thou mightst live!
My heart with anger and with pity bleeds.
Ah, bitter thought! Thy children fought and fell;
But not for dying Italy, ah, no,
But in the service of her cruel foe!

Father, if this enrage thee not,
How changed art thou from what thou wast on earth!
On Russia's plains, so bleak and desolate,
They died, the sons of Italy;
Ah, well deserving of a better fate!
In cruel war with men, with beasts,
The elements! In heaps they strewed the ground;
Half-clad, emaciated, stained with blood,
A bed of ice for their sick frames they found.
Then, when the parting hour drew near,
In fond remembrance of that mother dear,
They cried: "Oh had we fallen by the foeman's hand,
And not the victims of the clouds and storms,
And for *thy* good, our native land!
Now, far from thee, and in the bloom of youth,
Unknown to all, we yield our parting breath,
And die for *her*, who caused our country's death!"

The northern desert and the whispering groves,
Sole witnesses of their lament,
As thus they passed away!
And their neglected corpses, as they lay
Upon that horrid sea of snow exposed,
Were by the beasts consumed;
The memories of the brave and good,

And of the coward and the vile,
Unto the same oblivion doomed!
Dear souls, though infinite your wretchedness,
Rest, rest in peace! And yet what peace is yours,
Who can no comfort ever know
While Time endures!
Rest in the depths of your unmeasured woe,
O ye, *her* children true,
Whose fate alone with hers may vie,
In endless, hopeless misery!

But she rebukes you not,
Ah, no, but these alone,
Who forced you with her to contend;
And still her bitter tears she blends with yours,
In wretchedness that knows no end.
Oh that some pity in the heart were born,
For her, who hath all other glories won,
Of one, who from this dark, profound abyss,
Her weak and weary feet could guide!
Thou glorious shade, oh! say,
Does no one love thy Italy?
Say, is the flame that kindled thee extinct?
And will that myrtle never bloom again,
That hath so long consoled us in our pain?
Must all our garlands wither in the dust?
And shall we a redeemer never see,
Who may, in part, at least, resemble thee?

Are we forever lost?
Is there no limit to our shame?
I, while I live, will never cease to cry:
"Degenerate race, think of thy ancestry!
Behold these ruins vast,
These pictures, statues, temples, poems grand!
Think of the glories of thy native land!
If they thy soul cannot inspire or warn,
Why linger here? Arise! Begone!
This holy ground must not be thus defiled,
And must no shelter give
Unto the coward and the slave!
Far better were the silence of the grave!"

TO ANGELO MAI,

ON HIS DISCOVERY OF THE LOST BOOKS OF CICERO, "DE REPUBLICA."

Italian bold, why wilt thou never cease
The fathers from their tombs to summon forth?
Why bring them, with this dead age to converse,
That stifled is by enemies and by sloth?
And why dost thou, voice of our ancestors,
That hast so long been mute,
Resound so loud and frequent in our ears?
Why all these grand discoveries?
As in a flash the fruitful pages come,
What hath this wretched age deserved,
That dusty cloisters have for it reserved
These hidden treasures of the wise and brave?
Illustrious man, with what strange power
Does Fate thy ardent zeal befriend?
Or does Fate vainly with man's will contend?

Without the lofty counsel of the gods,
It surely could not be, that now,
When we were never sunk so low,
In desperate oblivion of the Past,
Each moment, comes a cry renewed,
From our great sires, to shake our souls, at last!
Heaven still some pity shows for Italy;
Some god hath still our happiness at heart:
Since this, or else no other, is the hour,
Italian virtue to redeem,
And its old lustre once more to impart,
These pleading voices from the grave we hear;
Forgotten heroes rise from earth again,
To see, my country, if at this late day,
Thou still art pleased the coward's part to play.

And do ye cherish still,
Illustrious shades, some hope of us?
Have we not perished utterly?
To you, perhaps, it is allowed, to read
The book of destiny. *I* am dismayed,

And have no refuge from my grief;
For dark to me the future is, and all
That I discern is such, as makes hope seem
A fable and a dream. To your old homes
A wretched crew succeed; to noble act or word,
They pay no heed; for your eternal fame
They know no envy, feel no blush of shame.
A filthy mob your monuments defile:
To ages yet unborn,
We have become a by-word and a scorn.

Thou noble spirit, if no others care
For our great Fathers' fame, oh, care thou still,
Thou, to whom Fate hath so benignant been,
That those old days appear again,
When, roused from dire oblivion's tomb,
Came forth, with all the treasures of their lore,
Those ancient bards, divine, with whom
Great Nature spake, but still behind her veil,
And with her mysteries graced
The holidays of Athens and of Rome.
O times, now buried in eternal sleep!
Our country's ruin was not then complete;
We then a life of wretched sloth disdained;
Still from our native soil were borne afar,
Some sparks of genius by the passing air.

Thy holy ashes still were warm,
Whom hostile fortune ne'er unmanned;
Unto whose anger and whose grief,
Hell was more grateful than thy native land.
Ah, what, but hell, has Italy become?
And thy sweet cords
Still trembled at the touch of thy right hand,
Unhappy bard of love.
Alas, Italian song is still the child
Of sorrow born.
And yet, less hard to bear,
Consuming grief than dull vacuity!
O blessed thou, whose life was one lament!
Disgust and nothingness are still our doom,
And by our cradle sit, and on our tomb.

But thy life, then, was with the stars and sea,
Liguria's hardy son,
When thou, beyond the columns and the shores,
Where oft, at set of sun,
The waves are heard to hiss,
As he into their depths has plunged,
Committed to the boundless deep,
Didst find again the sun's declining ray,
The new-born day didst find,
When it from us had passed away;
Defying Nature's every obstacle,
A land unknown didst win, the glorious spoils
Of all thy perils, all thy toils.
And yet, when known, the world seems smaller still;
And earth and ocean, and the heavenly sphere
More vast unto the child, than to the sage appear.

Where now are all the charming dreams
Of the mysterious retreats
Of dwellers unto us unknown,
Or where, by day, the stars to rest have gone,
Or of the couch remote of Eos bright,
Or of the sun's mysterious sleep at night?
They, in an instant, vanished all;
A little chart portrays this earthly ball.
Lo, all things are alike; discovery
But proves the way for dull vacuity.
Farewell to thee, O Fancy, dear,
If plain, unvarnished truth appear!
Thought more and more is still estranged from thee;
Thy power so mighty once, will soon be gone,
And our poor, wounded hearts be left forlorn.

But thou for these sweet dreams wast born,
And the *old* sun upon thee shone,
Delightful singer of the arms, and loves,
That in an age far happier than our own,
Men's lives with pleasing errors filled.
New hope of Italy! O towers, O caves,
O ladies, cavaliers,
O gardens, palaces! Amenites,
At thought of which, the mind
Is lost in thousand splendid reveries!

Ye lovely fables, and ye thoughts grotesque,
Now banished! And what to us remains?
Now that the bloom from all things is removed?
Alas, the sole, the certain thought,
That all except our wretchedness, is nought.

Torquato, O Torquato, heaven to us
The rich gift of thy genius gave, to thee
Nought else but misery.
Ill-starred Torquato, whom thy song,
So sweet, could not console,
Nor melt the ice, to which
The genial current of thy soul
Was turned, by private envy, princely hate;
And then, by Love abandoned, life's last dream!
To thee, nought real seemed but nothingness,
The world a dreary wilderness.
Too late the honors came, so long deferred;
And yet, to die was unto thee a gain.
Who knows the evils of our mortal state,
Demands but death, no garland asks, of Fate.

Return, return to us,
Rise from thy silent, dreary tomb,
And feast thine eyes on our distress,
O thou, whose life was crowned with wretchedness!
Far worse than what appeared to thee so sad
And infamous, have all our lives become.
Dear friend, who now would pity thee,
When none save for himself hath thought or care?
Who would not thy keen anguish folly call,
When all things great and rare the name of folly bear?
When envy, no, but worse than envy, far,
Indifference pervades our rulers all?
Ah, who would now, when we all think
Of song so little, and so much of gain,
A laurel for thy brow prepare again?

Ah, since thy day, there has appeared but one,
Who has the fame of Italy redeemed:
Too good for his vile age, he stands alone;
One of the fierce Allobroges,
Whose manly virtue was derived

Direct from heavenly powers,
Not from this dry, unfruitful earth of ours;
Whence he alone, unarmed,—
O matchless courage!—from the stage,
Did war upon the ruthless tyrants wage;
The only war, the only weapon left,
Against the crimes and follies of the age.
First, and alone, he took the field:
None followed him; all else were cowards tame,
Lost to all sense of honor, or of shame.

Devoured by anger and by grief,
His spotless life he passed,
Till from worse scenes released by death, at last.
O my Victorio, this was not for thee
The fitting age, or land.
Great souls congenial times and climes demand.
In mere repose we live content,
And vulgar mediocrity;
The wise man sinks, the mob ascends,
Till all at last in one dread level ends.
Go on, thou great discoverer!
Revive the dead, since all the living sleep!
Dead tongues of ancient heroes arm anew;
Till this vile age a new life strive to win
By noble deeds, or perish in its sin!

TO HIS SISTER PAOLINA,

ON HER APPROACHING MARRIAGE.

Since now thou art about to leave
Thy father's quiet house,
And all the phantoms and illusions dear,
That heaven-born fancies round it weave,
And to this lonely region lend their charm,
Unto the dust and noise of life condemned,
By destiny, soon wilt thou learn to see
Our wretchedness and infamy,
My sister dear, who, in these mournful times,
Alas, wilt more unhappy souls bestow
On our unhappy Italy!
With strong examples strengthen thou their minds;
For cruel fate propitious gales
Hath e'er to virtue's course denied,
Nor in weak souls can purity reside.

Thy sons must either poor, or cowards be.
Prefer them poor. It is the custom still.
Desert and fortune never yet were friends;
The strife between them never ends.
Unhappy they, who in these evil days
Are born when all things totter to their fall!
But that we must to heaven leave.
Be this, above all things, thy care,
Thy children still to rear,
As those who court not Fortune's smiles,
Nor playthings are of idle hope, or fear:
And so the future age will call them blessed;
For, in this slothful and deceitful world,
The living virtue ever we despise,
The dead we load with eulogies.

Women, to you our country looks,
For the redemption of her fame:
Ah, not unto our injury and shame,
On the soft lustre of your eyes
A power far mightier was conferred
Than that of fire or sword!

The wise and strong, in thought and act, are by
Your judgment led; nay all who live
Beneath the sun, to you still bend the knee.
On you I call, then; answer me!
Have *you* youth's holy aspirations quenched?
And are our natures broken, crushed by *you*?
These sluggish minds, these low desires,
These nerveless arms, these feeble knees.
Say, say, are you to blame for these?

Love is the spur to noble deeds,
To him its worth who knows;
And beauty still to lofty love inspires.
Love never in his spirit glows,
Whose heart exults not in his breast,
When angry winds in fight descend,
And heaven gathers all its clouds,
And mountain crests the lightnings rend.
O wives, O maidens, he
Who shrinks from danger, turns his back upon
His country in her need, and only seeks
His base desires and appetites to feed,
Excites your hatred and your scorn;
If ye for men, and not for milk-sops, feel
The glow of love o'er your soft bosoms steal.

The mothers of unwarlike sons
O may ye ne'er be called!
Your children still inure
For virtue's sake all trials to endure;
To scorn the vices of this wretched age;
To cherish loyal thoughts, and high desires;
And learn how much they owe unto their sires.
The sons of Sparta thus became,
Amid the memories of heroes old,
Deserving of the Grecian name;
While the young spouse the trusty sword
Upon the loved one's side would gird,
And, afterwards, with her black locks,
The bloodless, naked corpse concealed,
When homeward borne upon the faithful shield.

Virginia, thy soft cheek

In Beauty's finest mould was framed;
But thy disdain Rome's haughty lord inflamed.
How lovely wast thou, in thy youth's sweet prime,
When the rough dagger of thy sire
Thy snowy breast did smite,
And thou, a willing victim, didst descend
Into realms of night!
"May old age wither and consume my frame,
O father,"—thus she said;
"And may they now for me the tomb prepare,
E'er I the impious bed
Of that foul tyrant share:
And if my blood new life and liberty
May give to Rome, by thy hand let me die!"

Ah, in those better days
When more propitious shone the sun than now,
Thy tomb, dear child, was not left comfortless,
But honored with the tears of all.
Behold, around thy lovely corpse, the sons
Of Romulus with holy wrath inflamed;
Behold the tyrants locks with dust besmeared;
In sluggish breasts once more
The sacred name of Liberty revered;
Behold o'er all the subjugated earth,
The troops of Latium march triumphant forth,
From torrid desert to the gloomy pole.
And thus eternal Rome,
That had so long in sloth oblivious lain,
A daughter's sacrifice revives again.

TO A VICTOR IN THE GAME OF PALLONE.

The face of glory and her pleasant voice,
O fortunate youth, now recognize,
And how much nobler than effeminate sloth
Are manhood's tested energies.
Take heed, O generous champion, take heed,
If thou thy name by worthy thought or deed,
From Time's all-sweeping current couldst redeem;
Take heed, and lift thy heart to high desires!
The amphitheatre's applause, the public voice,
Now summon thee to deeds illustrious;
Exulting in thy lusty youth.
In thee, to-day, thy country dear
Beholds her heroes old again appear.

His hand was ne'er with blood barbaric stained,
At Marathon,
Who on the plain of Elis could behold
The naked athletes, and the wrestlers bold,
And feel no glow of emulous zeal within,
The laurel wreath of victory to win.
And he, who in Alpheus stream did wash
The dusty manes and foaming flanks
Of his victorious mares, *he* best could lead
The Grecian banners and the Grecian swords
Against the flying, panic-stricken ranks
Of Medes, who, dying, Asia's shore
And great Euphrates will behold no more.

And will you call that vain, which seeks
The latent sparks of virtue to evolve,
Or animate anew to high resolve,
The drooping fervor of our weary souls?
What but a game have mortal works e'er been,
Since Phoebus first his weary wheels did urge?
And is not truth, no less than falsehood, vain?
And yet, with pleasing phantoms, fleeting shows,
Nature herself to our relief has come;
And custom, aiding nature, still must strive
These strong illusions to revive;
Or else all thirst for noble deeds is gone,

Is lost in sloth, and blind oblivion.

The time may come, perchance, when midst
The ruins of Italian palaces,
Will herds of cattle graze,
And all the seven hills the plough will feel;
Not many years will have elapsed, perchance,
E'er all the towns of Italy
Will the abode of foxes be,
And dark groves murmur 'mid the lofty walls;
Unless the Fates from our perverted minds
Remove this sad oblivion of the Past;
And heaven by grateful memories appeased,
Relenting, in the hour of our despair,
The abject nations, ripe for slaughter, spare.

But thou, O worthy youth, wouldst grieve,
Thy wretched country to survive.
Thou once through her mightst have acquired renown,
When on her brow she wore the glittering crown,
Now lost! Our fault, and Fate's! That time is o'er;
Ah, such a mother who could honor, more?
But for thyself, O lift thy thoughts on high!
What is our life? A thing to be despised:
Least wretched, when with perils so beset,
It must, perforce, its wretched self forget,
Nor heed the flight of slow-paced, worthless hours;
Or, when, to Lethe's dismal shore impelled,
It hath once more the light of day beheld.

THE YOUNGER BRUTUS.

When in the Thracian dust uprooted lay,
In ruin vast, the strength of Italy,
And Fate had doomed Hesperia's valleys green,
And Tiber's shores,
The trampling of barbarian steeds to feel,
And from the leafless groves,
On which the Northern Bear looks down,
Had called the Gothic hordes,
That Rome's proud walls might fall before their swords;
Exhausted, wet with brothers' blood,
Alone sat Brutus, in the dismal night;
Resolved on death, the gods implacable
Of heaven and hell he chides,
And smites the listless, drowsy air
With his fierce cries of anger and despair.

"O foolish virtue, empty mists,
The realms of shadows, are thy schools,
And at thy heels repentance follows fast.
To you, ye marble gods
(If ye in Phlegethon reside, or dwell
Above the clouds), a mockery and scorn
Is the unhappy race,
Of whom you temples ask,
And fraudulent the law that you impose.
Say, then, does earthly piety provoke
The anger of the gods?
O Jove, dost thou protect the impious?
And when the storm-cloud rushes through the air,
And thou thy thunderbolts dost aim,
Against the *just* dost thou impel the sacred flame?
Unconquered Fate and stern necessity
Oppress the feeble slaves of Death:
Unable to avert their injuries,
The common herd endure them patiently.
But is the ill less hard to bear,
Because it has no remedy?
Does he who knows no hope no sorrow feel?
The hero wages war with thee,
Eternal deadly war, ungracious Fate,

And knows not how to yield; and thy right hand,
Imperious, proudly shaking off,
E'en when it weighs upon him most,
Though conquered, is triumphant still,
When his sharp sword inflicts the fatal blow;
And seeks with haughty smile the shades below.

"Who storms the gates of Tartarus,
Offends the gods.
Such valor does not suit, forsooth,
Their soft, eternal bosoms; no?
Or are our toils and miseries,
And all the anguish of our hearts,
A pleasant sport, their leisure to beguile?
Yet no such life of crime and wretchedness,
But pure and free as her own woods and fields,
Nature to us prescribed; a queen
And goddess once. Since impious custom, now,
Her happy realm hath scattered to the winds,
And other laws on this poor life imposed,
Will Nature of fool-hardiness accuse
The manly souls, who such a life refuse?

"Of crime, and their own sufferings ignorant,
Serene old age the beasts conducts
Unto the death they ne'er foresee.
But if, by misery impelled, they sought
To dash their heads against the rugged tree,
Or, plunging headlong from the lofty rock,
Their limbs to scatter to the winds.
No law mysterious, misconception dark,
Would the sad wish refuse to grant.
Of all that breathe the breath of life,
You, only, children of Prometheus, feel
That life a burden hard to bear;
Yet, would you seek the silent shores of death,
If sluggish fate the boon delay,
To you, alone, stern Jove forbids the way.

"And thou, white moon, art rising from the sea,
That with our blood is stained;
The troubled night dost thou survey,
And field, so fatal unto Italy.

On brothers' breasts the conqueror treads;
The hills with fear are thrilled;
From her proud heights Rome totters to her fall.
And smilest thou upon the dismal scene?
Lavinia's children from their birth,
And all their prosperous years,
And well-earned laurels, hast thou seen;
And thou *wilt* smile, with ray unchanged,
Upon the Alps, when, bowed with grief and shame,
The haughty city, desolate and lone,
Beneath the tread of Gothic hordes shall groan.

"Behold, amid the naked rocks,
Or on the verdant bough, the beast and bird,
Whose breasts are ne'er by thought or memory stirred,
Of the vast ruin take no heed,
Or of the altered fortunes of the world;
And when the humble herdsman's cot
Is tinted with the earliest rays of dawn,
The one will wake the valleys with his song,
The other, o'er the cliffs, the frightened throng
Of smaller beasts before him drive.
O foolish race! Most wretched we, of all!
Nor are these blood-stained fields,
These caverns, that our groans have heard,
Regardful of our misery;
Nor shines one star less brightly in the sky.
Not the deaf kings of heaven or hell,
Or the unworthy earth,
Or night, do I in death invoke,
Or thee, last gleam the dying hour that cheers,
The voice of coming ages. I no tomb
Desire, to be with sobs disturbed, or with
The words and gifts of wretched fools adorned.
The times grow worse and worse;
And who, unto a vile posterity,
The honor of great souls would trust,
Or fit atonement for their wrongs?
Then let the birds of prey around me wheel:
And let my wretched corpse
The lightning blast, the wild beast tear;
And let my name and memory melt in air!"

TO THE SPRING.

OR OF THE FABLES OF THE ANCIENTS.

Now that the sun the faded charms
Of heaven again restores,
And gentle zephyr the sick air revives,
And the dark shadows of the clouds
Are put to flight,
And birds their naked breasts confide
Unto the wind, and the soft light,
With new desire of love, and with new hope,
The conscious beasts, in the deep woods,
Amid the melting frosts, inspires;
May not to you, poor human souls,
Weary, and overborne with grief,
The happy age return, which misery,
And truth's dark torch, before its time, consumed?
Have not the golden rays
Of Phoebus vanished from your gaze
Forever? Say, O gentle Spring,
Canst thou this icy heart inspire, and melt,
That in the bloom of youth, the frost of age hath felt?

O holy Nature, art thou still alive?
Alive? And does the unaccustomed ear
Of thy maternal voice the accents hear?
Of white nymphs once, the streams were the abode.
And in the clear founts mirrored were their forms.
Mysterious dances of immortal feet
The mountain tops and lofty forests shook,—
To-day the lonely mansions of the winds;—
And when the shepherd-boy the noontide shade
Would seek, or bring his thirsty lambs
Unto the flowery margin of the stream,
Along the banks the clear song would he hear,
And pipe of rustic Fauns;
Would see the waters move,
And stand amazed, when, hidden from the view,
The quiver-bearing goddess would descend
Into the genial waves,
And from her snow-white arms efface

The dust and blood of the exciting chase.

The flowers, the herbs *once* lived,
The groves with life were filled:
Soft airs, and clouds, and every shining light
Were with the human race in sympathy,
When thee, fair star of Venus, o'er
The hills and dales,
The traveller, in the lonely night,
Pursuing with his earnest gaze,
The sweet companion of his path,
The loving friend of mortals deemed:
When he, who, fleeing from the impious strife
Of cities filled with mutiny and shame,
In depths of woods remote,
The rough trees clasping to his breast,
The vital flame seemed in their veins to feel,
The breathing leaves of Daphne, or of Phyllis sad;
And seemed the sisters' tears to see, still shed
For him who, smitten by the lightning's blast,
Into the swift Eridanus was cast.

Nor were ye deaf, ye rigid rocks,
To human sorrow's plaintive tones,
While in your dark recesses Echo dwelt,
No idle plaything of the winds,
But spirit sad of hapless nymph,
Whom unrequited love, and cruel fate,
Of her soft limbs deprived. She o'er the grots,
The naked rocks, and mansions desolate,
Unto the depths of all-embracing air,
Our sorrows, not to her unknown,
Our broken, loud laments conveyed.
And *thou*, if fame belie thee not,
Didst sound the depths of human woe,
Sweet bird, that comest to the leafy grove,
The new-born Spring to greet,
And when the fields are hushed in sleep,
To chant into the dark and silent air,
The ancient wrongs, and cruel treachery,
That stirred the pity of the gods, to see.
But, no, thy race is not akin to ours;
No sorrow framed thy melodies;

Thy voice of crime unconscious, pleases less,
Along the dusky valley heard.
Ah, since the mansions of Olympus all
Are desolate, and without guide, the bolt,
That, wandering o'er the cloud-capped mountain-tops,
In horror cold dissolves alike
The guilty and the innocent;
Since this, our earthly home,
A stranger to her children has become,
And brings them up, to misery;
Lend thou an ear, dear Nature, to the woes
And wretched fate of mortals, and revive
The ancient spark within my breast;
If thou, indeed, dost live, if aught there is,
In heaven, or on the sun-lit earth,
Or in the bosom of the sea,
That pities? No; but *sees* our misery.

HYMN TO THE PATRIARCHS.

OR OF THE BEGINNINGS OF THE HUMAN RACE.

Illustrious fathers of the human race,
Of you, the song of your afflicted sons
Will chant the praise; of you, more dear, by far,
Unto the Great Disposer of the stars,
Who were not born to wretchedness, like ours.
Immedicable woes, a life of tears,
The silent tomb, eternal night, to find
More sweet, by far, than the ethereal light,
These things were not by heaven's gracious law
Imposed on you. If ancient legends speak
Of sins of yours, that brought calamity
Upon the human race, and fell disease,
Alas, the sins more terrible, by far,
Committed by your children, and their souls
More restless, and with mad ambition fixed,
Against them roused the wrath of angry gods,
The hand of all-sustaining Nature armed,
By them so long neglected and despised.
Then life became a burden and a curse,
And every new-born babe a thing abhorred,
And hell and chaos reigned upon the earth.

Thou first the day, and thou the shining lights
Of the revolving stars didst see, the fields,
And their new flocks and herds, O leader old
And father of the human family!
The wandering air that o'er the meadows played,
When smote the rocks, and the deserted vales,
The torrent, rustling headlong from the Alps,
With sound, till then, unheard; and o'er the sites
Of future nations, noisy cities, yet unknown
To fame, a peace profound, mysterious reigned;
And o'er the unploughed hills, in silence, rose
The ray of Phoebus, and the golden moon.
O world, how happy in thy loneliness,
Of crimes and of disasters ignorant!
Oh, how much wretchedness Fate had in store
For thy poor race, unhappy father, what

A series vast of terrible events!
Behold, the fields, scarce tilled, with blood are stained,
A brother's blood, in sudden frenzy shed;
And now, alas, first hears the gentle air
The whirring of the fearful wings of Death.
The trembling fratricide, a fugitive,
The lonely shades avoids; in every blast
That sweeps the groves, a voice of wrath he hears.
He the first city builds, abode and realm
Of wasting cares; repentance desperate,
Heart-sick, and groaning, thus unites and binds
Together blind and sinful souls, and first
A refuge offers unto mutual guilt.
The wicked hand now scorns the crooked plough;
The sweat of honest labor is despised;
Now sloth possession of the threshold takes;
The sluggish frames their native vigor lose;
The minds in hopeless indolence are sunk;
And slavery, the crowning curse of all,
Degrades and crushes poor humanity.

And thou from heaven's wrath, and ocean's waves,
That bellowed round the cloud-capped mountain-tops,
The sinful brood didst save; thou, unto whom,
From the dark air and wave-encumbered hills,
The white dove brought the sign of hope renewed,
And sinking in the west, the shipwrecked sun,
His bright rays darting through the angry clouds,
The dark sky painted with the lovely bow.
The race restored, to earth returned, begins anew
The same career of wickedness and lust,
With their attendant ills. Audacious man
Defies the threats of the avenging sea,
And to new shores and to new stars repeats
The same sad tale of infamy and woe.

And now of thee I think, the just and brave,
The Father of the faithful, and the sons
Thy honored name that bore. Of thee I speak,
Whom, sitting, thoughtful, in the noontide shade,
Before thy humble cottage, near the banks,
That gave thy flocks both rest and nourishment,
The minds ethereal of celestial guests

With blessings greeted; and of thee, O son
Of wise Rebecca, how at eventide,
In Aran's valley sweet, and by the well,
Where happy swains in friendly converse met,
Thou didst with Laban's daughter fall in love;
Love, that to exile long, and suffering,
And to the odious yoke of servitude,
Thy patient soul a willing martyr led.

Oh, surely once,—for not with idle tales
And shadows, the Aonian song, and voice
Of Fame, the eager list'ners feed,—once was
This wretched earth more friendly to our race,
Was more beloved and dear, and golden flew
The days, that now so laden are with care.
Not that the milk, in waves of purest white,
Gushed from the rocks, and flowed along the vales;
Or that the tigers mingled with the sheep,
To the same fold were led; or shepherd-boys
With playful wolves would frolic at the spring;
But of its own lot ignorant, and all
The sufferings that were in store, devoid
Of care it lived: a soft, illusive veil
Of error hid the stern realities,
The cruel laws of heaven and of fate.
Life glided on, with cheerful hope content;
And tranquil, sought the haven of its rest.

So lives, in California's forests vast,
A happy race, whose life-blood is not drained
By pallid care, whose limbs are not by fierce
Disease consumed: the woods their food, their homes
The hollow rock, the streamlet of the vale
Its waters furnishes, and, unforeseen,
Dark death upon them steals. Ah, how unarmed,
Wise Nature's happy votaries, are ye,
Against our impious audacity!
Our fierce, indomitable love of gain
Your shores, your caves, your quiet woods invades;
Your minds corrupts, your bodies enervates;
And happiness, a naked fugitive,
Before it drives, to earth's remotest bounds.

THE LAST SONG OF SAPPHO.

Thou tranquil night, and thou, O gentle ray
Of the declining moon; and thou, that o'er
The rock appearest, 'mid the silent grove,
The messenger of day; how dear ye were,
And how delightful to these eyes, while yet
Unknown the furies, and grim Fate! But now,
No gentle sight can soothe this wounded soul.
Then, only, can forgotten joy revive,
When through the air, and o'er the trembling fields
The raging south wind whirls its clouds of dust;
And when the car, the pondrous car of Jove,
Omnipotent, high-thundering o'er our heads,
A pathway cleaves athwart the dusky sky.
Then would I love with storm-charged clouds to fly
Along the cliffs, along the valleys deep,
The headlong flight of frightened flocks to watch,
Or hear, upon some swollen river's shore
The angry billows' loud, triumphant roar.

How beautiful thou art, O heaven divine,
And thou, O dewy earth! Alas no part
Of all this beauty infinite, the gods
And cruel fate to wretched Sappho gave!
To thy proud realms, O Nature, I, a poor,
Unwelcome guest, rejected lover, come;
To all thy varied forms of loveliness,
My heart and eyes, a suppliant, lift in vain.
The sun-lit shore hath smiles no more for me,
Nor radiant morning light at heaven's gate;
The birds no longer greet me with their songs,
Nor whispering trees with gracious messages;
And where, beneath the bending willows' shade,
The limpid stream its bosom pure displays,
As I, with trembling and uncertain foot,
Oppressed with grief, upon its margin pause,
The dimpled waves recoil, as in disdain,
And urge their flight along the flowery plain.

What fearful crime, what hideous excess
Have so defiled me, e'en before my birth,

That heaven and fortune frown upon me thus?
Wherein have I offended, as a child,
When we of evil deeds are ignorant,
That thus disfigured, of the bloom of youth
Bereft, my little thread of life has from
The spindle of the unrelenting Fate
Been drawn? Alas, incautious are thy words!
Mysterious counsels all events control,
And all, except our grief, is mystery.
Deserted children, we were born to weep;
But why, is known to those above, alone.
O vain the cares, the hopes of earlier years!
To idle shows Jove gives eternal sway
O'er human hearts. Unless in shining robes arrayed,
All manly deeds in arms, or art, or song,
Appeal in vain unto the vulgar throng.

I die! This wretched veil to earth I cast,
And for my naked soul a refuge seek
Below, and for the cruel faults atone
Of gods, the blind dispensers of events.
And thou, to whom I have been bound so long,
By hopeless love, and lasting faith, and by
The frenzy vain of unappeased desire,
Live, live, and if thou canst, be happy here!
My cup o'erflows with bitterness, and Jove
Has from his vase no drop of sweetness shed,
For all my childhood's hopes and dreams have fled.
The happiest day the soonest fades away;
And then succeed disease, old age, the shade
Of icy death. Behold, alas! Of all
My longed-for laurels, my illusions dear,
The end,—the gulf of hell! My spirit proud
Must to the realm of Proserpine descend,
The Stygian shore, the night that knows no end.

FIRST LOVE.

Ah, well can I the day recall, when first
The conflict fierce of love I felt, and said:
If *this* be love, how hard it is to bear!

With eyes still fixed intent upon the ground,
I saw but *her*, whose artless innocence,
Triumphant took possession of this heart.

Ah, Love, how badly hast thou governed me!
Why should affection so sincere and pure,
Bring with it such desire, such suffering?

Why not serene, and full, and free from guile
But sorrow-laden, and lamenting sore,
Should joy so great into my heart descend?

O tell me, tender heart, that sufferest so,
Why with that thought such anguish should be blent,
Compared with which, all other thoughts were naught?

That thought, that ever present in the day,
That in the night more vivid still appeared,
When all things round in sweet sleep seemed to rest:

Thou, restless, both with joy and misery
Didst with thy constant throbbings weary so
My breast, as panting in my bed I lay.

And when worn out with grief and weariness,
In sleep my eyes I closed, ah, no relief
It gave, so broken and so feverish!

How brightly from the depths of darkness, then,
The lovely image rose, and my closed eyes,
Beneath their lids, their gaze upon it fed!

O what delicious impulses, diffused,
My weary frame with sweet emotion filled!
What myriad thoughts, unstable and confused,

Were floating in my mind! As through the leaves
Of some old grove, the west wind, wandering,
A long, mysterious murmur leaves behind.

And as I, silent, to their influence yield,
What saidst thou, heart, when she departed, who
Had caused thee all thy throbs, and suffering?

No sooner had I felt within, the heat
Of love's first flame, than with it flew away
The gentle breeze, that fanned it into life.

Sleepless I lay, until the dawn of day;
The steeds, that were to leave me desolate,
Their hoofs were beating at my father's gate.

And I, in mute suspense, poor timid fool,
With eye that vainly would the darkness pierce,
And eager ear intent, lay, listening,

That voice to hear, if, for the last time, I
Might catch the accents from those lovely lips;
The voice alone; all else forever lost!

How many vulgar tones my doubtful ear
Would smite, with deep disgust inspiring me,
With doubt tormented, holding hard my breath!

And when, at last, that voice into my heart
Descended, passing sweet, and when the sound
Of horses and of wheels had died away;

In utter desolation, then, my head
I in my pillow buried, closed my eyes,
And pressed my hand against my heart, and sighed.

Then, listlessly, my trembling knees across
The silent chamber dragging, I exclaimed,
"Nothing on earth can interest me more!"

The bitter recollection cherishing
Within my breast, to every voice my heart,
To every face, insensible remained.

Long I remained in hopeless sorrow drowned;
As when the heavens far and wide their showers
Incessant pour upon the fields around.

Nor had I, Love, thy cruel power known,
A boy of eighteen summers flown, until
That day, when I thy bitter lesson learned;

When I each pleasure held in scorn, nor cared
The shining stars to see, or meadows green,
Or felt the charm of holy morning light;

The love of glory, too, no longer found
An echo in my irresponsive breast,
That, once, the love of beauty with it shared.

My favorite studies I neglected quite;
And those things vain appeared, compared with which,
I used to think all other pleasures vain.

Ah! how could I have changed so utterly?
How could one passion all the rest destroy?
Indeed, what helpless mortals are we all!

My heart my only comfort was, and with
That heart, in conference perpetual,
A constant watch upon my grief to keep.

My eye still sought the ground, or in itself
Absorbed, shrank from encountering the glance
Of lovely or unlovely countenance;

The stainless image fearing to disturb,
So faithfully reflected in my breast;
As winds disturb the mirror of the lake.

And that regret, that I could not enjoy
Such happiness, which weighs upon the mind,
And turns to poison pleasure that has passed,

Did still its thorn within my bosom lodge,
As I the past recalled; but shame, indeed,
Left not its cruel sting within this heart.

To heaven, to you, ye gentle souls, I swear,
No base desire intruded on my thought;
But with a pure and sacred flame I burned.

That flame still lives, and that affection pure;
Still in my thought that lovely image breathes,
From which, save heavenly, I no other joy,

Have ever known; my only comfort, now!

THE LONELY SPARROW.

Thou from the top of yonder antique tower,
O lonely sparrow, wandering, hast gone,
Thy song repeating till the day is done,
And through this valley strays the harmony.
How Spring rejoices in the fields around,
And fills the air with light,
So that the heart is melted at the sight!
Hark to the bleating flocks, the lowing herds!
In sweet content, the other birds
Through the free sky in emulous circles wheel,
In pure enjoyment of their happy time:
Thou, pensive, gazest on the scene apart,
Nor wilt thou join them in the merry round;
Shy playmate, thou for mirth hast little heart;
And with thy plaintive music, dost consume
Both of the year, and of thy life, the bloom.

Alas, how much my ways
Resemble thine! The laughter and the sport,
That fill with glee our youthful days,
And thee, O love, who art youth's brother still,
Too oft the bitter sigh of later years,
I care not for; I know not why,
But from them ever distant fly:
Here in my native place,
As if of alien race,
My spring of life I like a hermit pass.
This day, that to the evening now gives way,
Is in our town an ancient holiday.
Hark, through the air, that voice of festal bell,
While rustic guns in frequent thunders sound,
Reverberated from the hills around.
In festal robes arrayed,
The neighboring youth,
Their houses leaving, o'er the roads are spread;
They pleasant looks exchange, and in their hearts
Rejoice. I, lonely, in this distant spot,
Along the country wandering,
Postpone all pleasure and delight
To some more genial time: meanwhile,

As through the sunny air around I gaze,
My brow is smitten by his rays,
As after such a day serene,
Dropping behind yon distant hills,
He vanishes, and seems to say,
That thus all happy youth must pass away.

Thou, lonely little bird, when thou
Hast reached the evening of the days
Thy stars assign to thee,
Wilt surely not regret thy ways;
For all thy wishes are
Obedient to Nature's law. But ah!
If I, in spite of all my prayers,
Am doomed the hateful threshold of old age
To cross, when these dull eyes will give
No response to another's heart,
The world to them a void will be,
Each day become more full of misery,
How then, will this, my wish appear
In those dark hours, that dungeon drear?
My blighted youth, my sore distress,
Alas, will *then* seem happiness!

THE INFINITE.

This lonely hill to me was ever dear,
This hedge, which shuts from view so large a part
Of the remote horizon. As I sit
And gaze, absorbed, I in my thought conceive
The boundless spaces that beyond it range,
The silence supernatural, and rest
Profound; and for a moment I am calm.
And as I listen to the wind, that through
These trees is murmuring, its plaintive voice
I with that infinite compare;
And things eternal I recall, and all
The seasons dead, and this, that round me lives,
And utters its complaint. Thus wandering
My thought in this immensity is drowned;
And sweet to me is shipwreck on this sea.

THE EVENING OF THE HOLIDAY.

The night is mild and clear, and without wind,
And o'er the roofs, and o'er the gardens round
The moon shines soft, and from afar reveals
Each mountain-peak serene. O lady, mine,
Hushed now is every path, and few and dim
The lamps that glimmer through the balconies.
Thou sleepest! in thy quiet rooms, how light
And easy is thy sleep! No care thy heart
Consumes; and little dost thou know or think,
How deep a wound thou in my heart hast made.
Thou sleepest; I to yonder heaven turn,
That seems to greet me with a loving smile,
And to that Nature old, omnipotent,
That doomed me still to suffer. "I to thee
All hope deny," she said, "e'en hope; nor may
Those eyes of thine e'er shine, save through their tears."

This was a holiday; its pleasures o'er,
Thou seek'st repose; and happy in thy dreams
Recallest those whom thou hast pleased to-day,
And those who have pleased thee: not I, indeed,—
I hoped it not,—unto thy thoughts occur.
Meanwhile, I ask, how much of life remains
To me; and on the earth I cast myself,
And cry, and groan. How wretched are my days,
And still so young! Hark, on the road I hear,
Not far away, the solitary song
Of workman, who returns at this late hour,
In merry mood, unto his humble home;
And in my heart a cruel pang I feel,
At thought, how all things earthly pass away,
And leave no trace behind. This festal day
Hath fled; a working-day now follows it,
And all, alike, are swept away by Time.
Where is the glory of the antique nations now?
Where now the fame of our great ancestors?
The empire vast of Rome, the clash of arms?
Now all is peace and silence, all the world
At rest; their very names are heard no more.
E'en from my earliest years, when we

Expect so eagerly a holiday,
The moment it was past, I sought my couch,
Wakeful and sad; and at the midnight hour,
When I the song heard of some passer-by,
That slowly in the distance died away,
The same deep anguish felt I in my heart.

TO THE MOON.

O lovely moon, how well do I recall
The time,—'tis just a year—when up this hill
I came, in my distress, to gaze at thee:
And thou suspended wast o'er yonder grove,
As now thou art, which thou with light dost fill.
But stained with mist, and tremulous, appeared
Thy countenance to me, because my eyes
Were filled with tears, that could not be suppressed;
For, oh, my life was wretched, wearisome,
And *is* so still, unchanged, beloved moon!
And yet this recollection pleases me,
This computation of my sorrow's age.
How pleasant is it, in the days of youth,
When hope a long career before it hath,
And memories are few, upon the past
To dwell, though sad, and though the sadness last!

THE DREAM.

It was the morning; through the shutters closed,
Along the balcony, the earliest rays
Of sunlight my dark room were entering;
When, at the time that sleep upon our eyes
Its softest and most grateful shadows casts,
There stood beside me, looking in my face,
The image dear of her, who taught me first
To love, then left me to lament her loss.
To me she seemed not dead, but sad, with such
A countenance as the unhappy wear.
Her right hand near my head she sighing placed;
"Dost thou still live," she said to me, "and dost
Thou still remember what we *were* and are?"
And I replied: "Whence comest thou, and how,
Beloved and beautiful? Oh how, how I
Have grieved, still grieve for thee! Nor did I think
Thou e'er couldst know it more; and oh, that thought
My sorrow rendered more disconsolate!
But art thou now again to leave me?
I fear so. Say, what hath befallen thee?
Art thou the same? What preys upon thee thus?"
"Oblivion weighs upon thy thoughts, and sleep
Envelops them," she answered; "I am dead,
And many months have passed, since last we met."
What grief oppressed me, as these words I heard!
And she continued: "In the flower of youth
Cut off, when life is sweetest, and before
The heart that lesson sad and sure hath learnt,
The utter vanity of human hope!
The sick man may e'en covet, as a boon,
That which withdraws him from all suffering;
But to the young, Death comes, disconsolate;
And hard the fate of hope, that in the grave
Is quenched! And yet, how vain that knowledge is,
That Nature from the inexperienced hides!
And a blind sorrow is to be preferred
To wisdom premature!"—"Hush, hush!" I cried,
"Unhappy one, and dear! My heart is crushed
With these thy words! And art thou dead, indeed,
O my beloved? and am I still alive?

And was it, then, in heaven decreed, that this,
Thy tender body the last damps of death
Should feel, and my poor, wretched frame remain
Unharmed? Oh, often, often as I think
That thou no longer livest, and that I
Shall never see thee on the earth again,
Incredible it seems! Alas, alas!
What *is* this thing, that they call death? Oh, would
That I, this day, the mystery could solve,
And my defenceless head withdraw from Fate's
Relentless hate! I still am young, and still
Feel all the blight and misery of age,
Which I so dread; and distant far it seems;
But, ah, how little different from age,
The flower of my years!"—"We both were born,"
She said, "to weep; unhappy were our lives,
And heaven took pleasure in our sufferings."
"Oh if my eyes with tears," I added, "then,
My face with pallor veiled thou seest, for loss
Of thee, and anguish weighing on my heart;
Tell me, was any spark of pity or of love
For the poor lover kindled in thy heart,
While thou didst live? I, then, between my hope
And my despair, passed weary nights and days;
And now, my mind is with vain doubts oppressed.
Oh if but once compassion smote thee for
My darkened life, conceal it not from me,
I pray thee; let the memory console me,
Since of their future our young days were robbed!"
And she: "Be comforted, unhappy one!
I was not churlish of my pity whilst
I lived, and am not now, myself so wretched!
Oh, do not chide this most unhappy child!"
"By all our sufferings, and by the love
Which preys upon me," I exclaimed, "and by
Our youth, and by the hope that faded from
Our lives, O let me, dearest, touch thy hand!"
And sweetly, sadly, she extended it.
And while I covered it with kisses, while
With sorrow and with rapture quivering,
I to my panting bosom fondly pressed it,
With fervent passion glowed my face and breast,
My trembling voice refused its utterance,

And all things swam before my sight; when she,
Her eyes fixed tenderly on mine, replied:
"And dost thou, then, forget, dear friend, that I
Am of my beauty utterly deprived?
And vainly thou, unhappy one, dost yield
To passion's transports. Now, a last farewell!
Our wretched minds, our feeble bodies, too,
Eternally are parted. Thou to me
No longer livest, nevermore shall live.
Fate hath annulled the faith that thou hast sworn."
Then, in my anguish as I seemed to cry
Aloud, convulsed, my eyes o'erflowing with
The tears of utter, helpless misery,
I started from my sleep. The image still
Was seen, and in the sun's uncertain light
Above my couch she seemed to linger still.

THE LONELY LIFE.

The morning rain, when, from her coop released,
The hen, exulting, flaps her wings, when from
The balcony the husbandman looks forth,
And when the rising sun his trembling rays
Darts through the falling drops, against my roof
And windows gently beating, wakens me.
I rise, and grateful, bless the flying clouds,
The cheerful twitter of the early birds,
The smiling fields, and the refreshing air.
For I of you, unhappy city walls,
Enough have seen and known; where hatred still
Companion is to grief; and grieving still
I live, and so shall die, and that, how soon!
But here some pity Nature shows, though small,
Once in this spot to me so courteous!
Thou, too, O Nature, turn'st away thy gaze
From misery; thou, too, thy sympathy
Withholding from the suffering and the sad,
Dost homage pay to royal happiness.
No friend in heaven, on earth, the wretched hath,
No refuge, save his trusty dagger's edge.
Sometimes I sit in perfect solitude,
Upon a hill, that overlooks a lake,
That is encircled quite with silent trees.
There, when the sun his mid-day course hath reached,
His tranquil face he in a mirror sees:
Nor grass nor leaf is shaken by the wind;
There is no ripple on the wave, no chirp
Of cricket, rustling wing of bird in bush,
Nor hum of butterfly; no motion, voice,
Or far or near, is either seen or heard.
Its shores are locked in quiet most profound;
So that myself, the world I quite forget,
As motionless I sit; my limbs appear
To lie dissolved, of breath and sense deprived;
As if, in immemorial rest, they seemed
Confounded with the silent scene around.

O love, O love, long since, thou from this breast
Hast flown, that was so warm, so ardent, once.

Misfortune in her cold and cruel grasp
Has held it fast, and it to ice has turned,
E'en in the flower of my youth. The time
I well recall, when thou this heart didst fill;
That sweet, irrevocable time it was,
When this unhappy scene of life unto
The ardent gaze of youth reveals itself,
Expands, and wears the smile of Paradise.
How throbs the heart within the boyish breast,
By virgin hope and fond desire impelled!
The wretched dupe for life's hard work prepares,
As if it were a dance, or merry game.
But when *I* first, O love, thy presence felt,
Misfortune had already crushed my life,
And these poor eyes with constant tears were filled.
Yet if, at times, upon the sun-lit slopes,
At silent dawn, or when, in broad noonday,
The roofs and hills and fields are shining bright,
I of some lonely maiden meet the gaze;
Or when, in silence of the summer night,
My wandering steps arresting, I before
The houses of the village pause, to gaze
Upon the lonely scene, and hear the voice,
So clear and cheerful, of the maiden, who,
Her ditty chanting, in her quiet room,
Her daily task protracts into the night,
Ah, then this stony heart will throb once more;
But soon, alas, its lethargy returns,
For all things sweet are strangers to this breast!

Beloved moon, beneath whose tranquil rays
The hares dance in the groves, and at the dawn
The huntsman, vexed at heart, beholds the tracks
Confused and intricate, that from their forms
His steps mislead; hail, thou benignant Queen
Of Night! How unpropitious fall thy rays,
Among the cliffs and thickets, or within
Deserted buildings, on the gleaming steel
Of robber pale, who with attentive ear
Unto the distant noise of horses and
Of wheels, is listening, or the tramp of feet
Upon the silent road; then, suddenly,
With sound of arms, and hoarse, harsh voice, and look

Of death, the traveller's heart doth chill,
Whom he half-dead, and naked, shortly leaves
Among the rocks. How unpropitious, too,
Is thy bright light along the city streets,
Unto the worthless paramour, who picks
His way, close to the walls, in anxious search
Of friendly shade, and halts, and dreads the sight
Of blazing lamps, and open balconies.
To evil spirits unpropitious still,
To *me* thy face will ever seem benign,
Along these heights, where nought save smiling hills,
And spacious fields, thou offer'st to my view.
And yet it was my wayward custom once,
Though I was innocent, thy gracious ray
To chide, amid the haunts of men, whene'er
It would my face to them betray, and when
It would their faces unto me reveal.
Now will I, grateful, sing its constant praise,
When I behold thee, sailing through the clouds,
Or when, mild sovereign of the realms of air,
Thou lookest down on this, our vale of tears.
Me wilt thou oft behold, mute wanderer
Among the groves, along the verdant banks,
Or seated on the grass, content enough,
If heart and breath are left me, for a sigh!

CONSALVO.

Approaching now the end of his abode
On earth, Consalvo lay; complaining once,
Of his hard fate, but now quite reconciled,
When, in the midst of his fifth lustre, o'er
His head oblivion, so longed-for, hung.
As for some time, so, on his dying day,
He lay, abandoned by his dearest friends:
For in the world, few friends to *him* will cling,
Who shows that he is weary of the world.
Yet *she* was at his side, by pity led,
In his lone wretchedness to comfort him,
Who was alone and ever in his thought;
Elvira, for her loveliness renowned;
And knowing well her power; that a look,
A single sweet and gracious word from *her*,
A thousand-fold repeated in the heart,
Devoted, of her hapless lover, still
His consolation and support had been,
Although no word of love had she from him
E'er heard. For ever in his soul the power
Of great desire had been rebuked and crushed
By sovereign fear. So great a child and slave
Had he become, through his excess of love!
But death at last the cruel silence broke;
For being by sure signs convinced, that now
The day of his deliverance had come,
Her white hand taking, as she was about
To leave, and gently pressing it, he said:
"Thou goest; it is time for thee to go;
Farewell, Elvira! I shall never see
Thee more; too well I know it; so, farewell!
I thank thee for thy gentle sympathy,
So far as my poor lips my thanks can speak.
He will reward thee, who alone has power,
If heaven e'er rewards the merciful."
Pale turned the fair one at these words; a sigh
Her bosom heaved; for e'en a stranger's heart
A throb responsive feels, when she departs,
And says farewell forever. Fain would she
Have contradicted him, the near approach

Of fate concealing from the dying man.
But he, her thought anticipating, said:
"Ah, much desired, as well thou knowest, death,
Much prayed for, and not dreaded, comes to me;
Nay, joyful seems to me this fatal day,
Save for the thought of losing thee forever;
Alas, forever do I part from thee!
In saying this my heart is rent in twain.
Those eyes I shall no more behold, nor hear
Thy voice. But, O Elvira, say, before
Thou leavest me forever, wilt thou not
One kiss bestow? A single kiss, in all
My life? A favor asked, who can deny
Unto a dying man? Of the sweet gift
I ne'er can boast, so near my end, whose lips
To-day will by a stranger's hand be closed
Forever." Saying this, with a deep sigh,
Her hand beloved he with his cold lips pressed.

The lovely woman stood irresolute,
And thoughtful, for a moment, with her look,
In which a thousand charms were radiant,
Intent on that of the unhappy man,
Where the last tear was glittering. Nor would
Her heart permit her to refuse with scorn
His wish, and by refusal, make more sad
The sad farewell; but she compassion took
Upon his love, which she had known so long;
And that celestial face, that mouth, which he
So long had coveted, which had, for years,
The burden been of all his dreams and sighs,
Close bringing unto his, so sad and wan,
Discolored by his mortal agony,
Kiss after kiss, all goodness, with a look
Of deep compassion, on the trembling lips
Of the enraptured lover she impressed.

What didst thou then become? How in thy eyes
Appeared life, death, and all thy suffering,
Consalvo, in thy flight now pausing? He
The hand, which still he held, of his beloved
Elvira, placing on his heart, whose last
Pulsations love with death was sharing, said:

"Elvira, my Elvira, am I still
On earth? Those lips, were they thy lips? O, say!
And do I press thy hand? Alas, it seems
A dead man's vision, or a dream, or thing
Incredible! How much, Elvira, O,
How much I owe to death! Long has my love
Been known to thee, and unto others, for
True love cannot be hidden on the earth.
Too manifest it was to thee, in looks,
In acts, in my unhappy countenance,
But never in my words. For then, and now,
Forever would the passion infinite,
That rules my heart, be silent, had not death
With courage filled it. I shall die content;
Henceforth, with destiny, no more regret
That I e'er saw the light. I have not lived
In vain, now that my lips have been allowed
Thy lips to press. Nay, happy I esteem
My lot. Two precious things the world still gives
To mortals, Love and Death. To one, heaven guides
Me now, in youth; and in the other, I
Am fortunate. Ah, hadst thou once, but once,
Responded to my long-enduring love,
To my changed eyes this earth for evermore
Had been transformed into a Paradise.
E'en to old age, detestable old age,
Could I have been resigned and reconciled.
To bear its heavy load, the memory
Of one transcendent moment had sufficed,
When I was happier than the happiest,
But, ah, such bliss supreme the envious gods
To earthly natures ne'er have given! Love
In such excess ne'er leads to happiness.
And yet, thy love to win, I would have borne
The tortures of the executioner;
Have faced the rack and fagot, dauntlessly;
Would from thy loving arms have rushed into
The fearful flames of hell, with cheerfulness.

"Elvira, O Elvira, happy he,
Beyond all mortal happiness, on whom
Thou dost the smile of love bestow! And next
Is he, who can lay down his life for thee!

It *is* permitted, it is not a dream,
As I, alas, have always fancied it,
To man, on earth true happiness to find.
I knew it well, the day I looked on thee.
That look to me, indeed, has fatal been:
And yet, I could not bring myself, midst all
My sufferings, that cruel day to blame.

"Now live, Elvira, happy, and adorn
The world with thy fair countenance. None e'er
Will love thee as I loved thee. Such a love
Will ne'er be seen on earth. How much, alas,
How long a time by poor Consalvo hast
Thou been with sighs and bitter tears invoked!
How, when I heard thy name, have I turned pale!
How have I trembled, and been sick at heart,
As timidly thy threshold I approached,
At that angelic voice, at sight of that
Fair brow, I, who now tremble not at death!
But breath and life no longer will respond
Unto the voice of love. The time has passed;
Nor can I e'er this happy day recall.
Farewell, Elvira! With its vital spark
Thy image so beloved is from my heart
Forever fading. Oh, farewell! If this,
My love offend thee not, to-morrow eve
One sigh wilt thou bestow upon my bier."
He ceased; and soon he lost his consciousness:
Ere evening came, his first, his only day
Of happiness had faded from his sight.

TO THE BELOVED.

Beauty beloved, who hast my heart inspired,
Seen from afar, or with thy face concealed,
Save, when in visions of the night revealed,
Or seen in daydreams bright,
When all the fields are filled with light,
And Nature's smile is sweet,
Say, hast thou blessed
Some golden age of innocence,
And floatest, now, a shadow, o'er the earth?
Or hath Fate's envious doom
Reserved thee for some happier day to come?

To see thee e'er alive,
No hope remains to me;
Unless perchance, when from this body free,
My wandering spirit, lone,
O'er some new path, to some new world hath flown.
E'en here, at first, I, at the dawn
Of this, my day, so dreary and forlorn,
Sought thee, to guide me on my weary way:
But none on earth resembles thee. E'en if
One were in looks and acts and words thy peer,
Though like thee, she less lovely would appear.

Amidst the deepest grief
That fate hath e'er to human lot assigned,
Could one but love thee on this earth,
Alive, and such as my thought painteth thee,
He would be happy in his misery:
And I most clearly see, how, still,
As in my earliest days,
Thy love would make me cling to virtue's ways.
Unto *my* grief heaven hath no comfort brought;
And yet with thee, this mortal life would seem
Like that in heaven, of which we fondly dream.

Along the valleys where is heard
The song of the laborious husbandman,
And where I sit and moan
O'er youth's illusions gone;

Along the hills, where I recall with tears,
The vanished joys and hopes of earlier years,
At thought of thee, my heart revives again.
O could I still thy image dear retain,
In this dark age, and in this baleful air!
To loss of thee, O let me be resigned,
And in thy image still some comfort find!

If thou art one of those
Ideas eternal, which the Eternal Mind
Refused in earthly form to clothe,
Nor would subject unto the pain and strife
Of this, our frail and dreary life;
Or if thou hast a mansion fair,
Amid the boundless realms of space,
That lighted is by a more genial sun,
And breathest there a more benignant air;
From here, where brief and wretched are our days,
Receive thy humble lover's hymn of praise!

TO COUNT CARLO PEPOLI.

This wearisome and this distressing sleep
That we call life, O how dost thou support,
My Pepoli? With what hopes feedest thou
Thy heart? Say in what thoughts, and in what deeds,
Agreeable or sad, dost thou invest
The idleness thy ancestors bequeathed
To thee, a dull and heavy heritage?
All life, indeed, in every walk of life,
Is idleness, if we may give that name
To every work achieved, or effort made,
That has no worthy aim in view, or fails
That aim to reach. And if you idle call
The busy crew, that daily we behold,
From tranquil morn unto the dewy eve,
Behind the plough, or tending plants and flocks,
Because they live simply to keep alive,
And life is worthless for itself alone,
The honest truth you speak. His nights and days
The pilot spends in idleness; the toil
And sweat in workshops are but idleness;
The soldier's vigils, perils of the field,
The eager merchant's cares are idle all;
Because true happiness, for which alone
Our mortal nature longs and strives, no man,
Or for himself, or others, e'er acquires
Through toil or sweat, through peril, or through care.
Yet for this fierce desire, which mortals still
From the beginning of the world have felt,
But ever felt in vain, for happiness,
By way of soothing remedy devised,
Nature, in this unhappy life of ours,
Had manifold necessities prepared,
Not without thought or labor satisfied;
So that the days, though ever sad, less dull
Might seem unto the human family;
And this desire, bewildered and confused,
Might have less power to agitate the heart.
So, too, the various families of brutes,
Who have, no less than we, and vainly, too,
Desire for happiness; but they, intent

On that which is essential to their life,
Consume their days more pleasantly, by far,
Nor chide, with us, the dulness of the hours.
But *we*, who unto other hands commit
The furnishing of our immediate wants,
Have a necessity more grave to meet,
For which no other ever can provide,
With ennui laden, and with suffering;
The stern necessity of killing time;
That cruel, obstinate necessity,
From which, nor hoarded gold, nor wealth of flocks,
Nor fertile fields, nor sumptuous palaces,
Nor purple robes, the race of man can save.
And if one, scorning such a barren life,
And hating to behold the light of day,
Turns not a homicidal hand upon
Himself, anticipating sluggish Fate,
For the sharp sting of unappeased desire,
That vainly calls for happiness, he seeks,
In desperate chase, on every side, in vain,
A thousand inefficient remedies,
In lieu of that, which Nature gives to all.

One to his dress devotes himself, and hair,
His gait and gesture and the learned lore
Of horses, carriages, to crowded halls,
To thronged piazzas, and to gardens gay;
Another gives his nights and days to games,
And feasts, and dances with the reigning belles:
A smile perpetual is on his lips;
But in his breast, alas, stern and severe,
Like adamantine column motionless,
Eternal ennui sits, against whose might
Avail not vigorous youth, nor prattle fond
That falls from rosy lips, nor tender glance
That trembles in two dark and lustrous eyes;
The most bewildering of mortal things,
Most precious gift of heaven unto man.

Another, as if hoping to escape
Sad destiny, in changing lands and climes
His days consuming, wandering o'er sea
And hills, the whole earth traverses; each spot

That Nature, in her infinite domain,
To restless man hath made accessible,
He visits in his wanderings. Alas,
Black care is seated on the lofty prow;
Beneath each clime, each sky, he asks in vain
For happiness; sadness still lives and reigns.

Another in the cruel deeds of war
Prefers to pass his hours, and dips his hand,
For his diversion, in his brother's blood:
Another in his neighbor's misery
His comfort finds, and artfully contrives
To kill the time, in making others sad.
This man still walks in wisdom's ways, or art
Pursues; *that* tramples on the people's rights,
At home, abroad; the ancient rest disturbs
Of distant shores, on fraudful gain intent,
With cruel war, or sharp diplomacy;
And so his destined part of life consumes.

Thee a more gentle wish, a care more sweet
Leads and controls, still in the flower of youth,
In the fair April of thy days, to most
A time so pleasant, heaven's choicest gift;
But heavy, bitter, wearisome to *him*
Who has no country. Thee the love of song
Impels, and of portraying in thy speech
The beauty, that so seldom in the world
Appears and fades so soon, and *that,* more rare
Which fond imagination, kinder far
Than Nature, or than heaven, so bounteously
For our entranced, deluded souls provides.
Oh, fortunate a thousand-fold is he,
Who loses not his fancy's freshness as
The years roll by; whom envious Fate permits
To keep eternal sunshine in his heart,
Who, in his ripe and his declining years,
As was his custom in his glorious youth,
In his deep thought enhances Nature's charms,
Gives life to death, and to the desert, bloom.
May heaven this fortune give to thee; and may
The spark that now so warms thy breast, make thee
In thy old age a votary of song!

I feel no more the sweet illusions of
That happy time; those charming images
Have faded from my eyes, that I so loved,
And which, unto my latest hour, will be
Remembered still, with hopeless sighs and tears.
And when this breast to all things has become
Insensible and cold, nor the sweet smile
And rest profound of lonely sun-lit plains,
Nor cheerful morning song of birds in spring,
Nor moonlight soft, that rests on hills and fields,
Beneath the limpid sky, will move my heart;
When every beauty, both of Nature, and
Of Art, to me will be inanimate
And mute; each tender feeling, lofty thought,
Unknown and strange; my only comfort, then,
Poor beggar, must I find in studies more
Severe; to them, thenceforward, must devote
The wretched remnant of unhappy life:
The bitter truth must I investigate,
The destinies mysterious, alike
Of mortal and immortal things;
For what was suffering humanity,
Bowed down beneath the weight of misery,
Created; to what final goal are Fate
And Nature urging it; to whom can our
Great sorrow any pleasure, profit give;
Beneath what laws and orders, to what end,
The mighty Universe revolves—the theme
Of wise men's praise, to *me* a mystery?

I in these speculations will consume
My idleness; because the truth, when known,
Though sad, has yet its charms. And if, at times,
The truth discussing, my opinions should
Unwelcome be, or not be understood,
I shall not grieve, indeed, because in me
The love of fame will be extinguished quite;
Of fame, that idol frivolous and blind;
More blind by far than Fortune, or than Love.

THE RESURRECTION.

I thought I had forever lost,
  Alas, though still so young,
The tender joys and sorrows all,
  That unto youth belong;

The sufferings sweet, the impulses
  Our inmost hearts that warm;
Whatever gives this life of ours
  Its value and its charm.

What sore laments, what bitter tears
  O'er my sad state I shed,
When first I felt from my cold heart
  Its gentle pains had fled!

Its throbs I felt no more; my love
  Within me seemed to die;
Nor from my frozen, senseless breast
  Escaped a single sigh!

I wept o'er my sad, hapless lot;
  The life of life seemed lost;
The earth an arid wilderness,
  Locked in eternal frost;

The day how dreary, and the night
  How dull, and dark, and lone!
The moon for me no brightness had,
  No star in heaven shone.

And yet the old love was the cause
  Of all the tears I shed;
Still in my inmost breast I felt
  The heart was not yet dead.

My weary fancy still would crave
  The images it loved,
And its capricious longings still
  A source of sorrow proved.

But e'en that lingering spark of grief
 Was soon within me spent,
And I the strength no longer had
 To utter a lament.

And there I lay, stunned, stupefied,
 Nor asked for comfort more;
My heart to hopeless, blank despair
 Itself had given o'er.

How changed, alas, was I from him
 Who once with passion thrilled,
Whose ardent soul was ever, once,
 With sweet illusions filled!

The swallow to my window, still,
 Would come, to greet the dawn;
But his sweet song no echo found
 In my poor heart, forlorn.

Nor pleased me more, in autumn gray,
 Upon the hill-side lone,
The cheerful vesper-bell, or light
 Of the departing sun.

In vain the evening star I saw
 Above the silent vale,
And vainly warbled in the grove
 The plaintive nightingale.

And you, ye furtive glances, bright,
 From gentle eyes that rove,
The sweet, the gracious messages
 Of first immortal Love;

The soft, white hand, that tenderly
 My own hand seemed to woo;
All, all your magic spells were vain,
 My torpor to subdue.

Of every pleasure quite bereft,
 Sad but of tranquil mien;
A state of perfect littleness,

  Yet with a face serene;

Save for the lingering wish, indeed,
  In death to sink to rest,
The force of all desire was spent
  In my exhausted breast.

As some poor, feeble wanderer,
  With age and sorrow bent,
The April of my years, alas,
  Thus listlessly I spent;

Thus listlessly, thus wearily,
  Didst thou consume, O heart,
Those golden days, ineffable,
  So swiftly that depart.

Who, from this heavy, heedless rest
  Awakens me again?
What new, what magic power is this,
  I feel within me reign?

Ye motions sweet, ye images,
  Ye throbs, illusions blest,
Ah, no,—ye are not then shut out
  Forever from this breast?

The glorious light of golden days
  Do ye again unfold?
The old affections that I lost,
  Do I once more behold?

Now, as I gaze upon the sky,
  Or on the verdant fields,
Each thing with sorrow me inspires,
  And each a pleasure yields.

The mountain, forest, and the shore
  Once more my heart rejoice;
The fountain speaks to me once more,
  The sea hath found a voice.

Who, after all this apathy,

Restores to me my tears?
Each moment, as I look around,
How changed the world appears!

Hath hope, perchance, O my poor heart,
Beguiled thee of thy pain?
Ah, no, the gracious smile of hope
I ne'er shall see again.

Nature bestowed these impulses,
And these illusions blest;
Their inborn influence, in me,
By suffering was suppressed;

But not annulled, not overcome
By cruel blows of Fate;
Nor by the inauspicious frown
Of Truth, importunate!

I know she has no sympathy
For fond imaginings;
I know that Nature, too, is deaf,
Nor heeds our sufferings;

That for our *good* she nothing cares,
Our *being*, only heeds;
And with the sight of our distress
Her wild caprices feeds.

I know the poor man pleads in vain,
For others' sympathy;
That scornfully, or heedlessly,
All from his presence flee;

That both for genius and for worth,
This age has no respect;
That all who cherish lofty aims
Are left to cold neglect.

And you, ye eyes so tremulous
With lustre all divine,
I know how false your splendors are,
Where no true love doth shine.

No love mysterious and profound
  Illumes you with its glow;
Nor gleams one spark of genial fire
  Beneath that breast of snow.

Nay, it is wont to laugh to scorn
  Another's tender pain;
The fervent flame of heavenly love
  To treat with cold disdain.

Yet I with thankfulness once more
  The old illusions greet,
And feel, with shock of pleased surprise,
  The heart within me beat.

To thee alone this force renewed,
  This vital power I owe;
From thee alone, my faithful heart,
  My only comforts flow.

I feel it is the destiny
  Of every noble mind,
In Fate, in Fortune, Beauty, and the World,
  An enemy to find:

But while thou liv'st, nor yield'st to Fate,
  Contending without fear,
I will not tax with cruelty
  The power that placed me here.

TO SYLVIA.

O Sylvia, dost thou remember still
That period of thy mortal life,
When beauty so bewildering
Shone in thy laughing, glancing eyes,
As thou, so merry, yet so wise,
Youth's threshold then wast entering?

How did the quiet rooms,
And all the paths around,
With thy perpetual song resound,
As thou didst sit, on woman's work intent,
Abundantly content
With the vague future, floating on thy mind!
Thy custom thus to spend the day
In that sweet time of youth and May!

How could I, then, at times,
In those fair days of youth,
The only happy days I ever knew,
My hard tasks dropping, or my careless rhymes,
My station take, on father's balcony,
And listen to thy voice's melody,
And watch thy hands, as they would deftly fly
O'er thy embroidery!
I gazed upon the heaven serene,
The sun-lit paths, the orchards green,
The distant mountain here,
And there, the far-off sea.
Ah, mortal tongue cannot express
What then I felt of happiness!

What gentle thoughts, what hopes divine,
What loving hearts, O Sylvia mine!
In what bright colors then portrayed
Were human life and fate!
Oh, when I think of such fond hopes betrayed,
A feeling seizes me
Of bitterness and misery,
And tenfold is my grief renewed!
O Nature, why this treachery?

Why thus, with broken promises,
Thy children's hearts delude?

Thou, ere the grass was touched with winter's frost,
By fell disease attacked and overcome,
O tender plant, didst die!
The flower of thy days thou ne'er didst see;
Nor did thy soft heart move
Now of thy raven locks the tender praise,
Now of thy eyes, so loving and so shy;
Nor with thee, on the holidays,
Did thy companions talk of love.

So perished, too, erelong,
My own sweet hope;
So too, unto my years
Did Fate their youth deny.
Alas, alas the day,
Lamented hope, companion dear,
How hast thou passed away!
Is *this* that world? These the delights,
The love, the labors, the events,
Of which we once so fondly spoke?
And must *all* mortals wear this weary yoke?
Ah, when the truth appeared,
It better seemed to die!
Cold death, the barren tomb, didst thou prefer
To harsh reality.

RECOLLECTIONS.

Ye dear stars of the Bear, I did not think
I should again be turning, as I used,
To see you over father's garden shine,
And from the windows talk with you again
Of this old house, where as a child I dwelt,
And where I saw the end of all my joys.
What charming images, what fables, once,
The sight of you created in my thought,
And of the lights that bear you company!
Silent upon the verdant clod I sat,
My evening thus consuming, as I gazed
Upon the heavens, and listened to the chant
Of frogs that in the distant marshes croaked;
While o'er the hedges, ditches, fire-flies roamed,
And the green avenues and cypresses
In yonder grove were murmuring to the wind;
While in the house were heard, at intervals,
The voices of the servants at their work.
What thoughts immense in me the sight inspired
Of that far sea, and of the mountains blue,
That yonder I behold, and which I thought
One day to cross, mysterious worlds and joys
Mysterious in the future fancying!
Of my hard fate unconscious, and how oft
This sorrowful and barren life of mine
I willingly would have for death exchanged!

Nor did my heart e'er tell me, I should be
Condemned the flower of my youth to spend
In this wild native region, and amongst
A wretched, clownish crew, to whom the names
Of wisdom, learning, are but empty sounds,
Or arguments of laughter and of scorn;
Who hate, avoid me; not from envy, no;
For they do not esteem me better than
Themselves, but fancy that I, in my heart,
That feeling cherish; though I strive, indeed,
No token of such feeling to display.
And here I pass my years, abandoned, lost,
Of love deprived, of life; and rendered fierce,

'Mid such a crowd of evil-minded ones,
My pity and my courtesy I lose,
And I become a scorner of my race,
By such a herd surrounded; meanwhile, fly
The precious hours of youth, more precious far
Than fame, or laurel, or the light of day,
Or breath of life: thus uselessly, without
One joy, I lose thee, in this rough abode,
Whose only guests are care and suffering,
O thou, the only flower of barren life!

The wind now from the tower of the town
The deep sound of the bell is bringing. Oh,
What comfort was that sound to me, a child,
When in my dark and silent room I lay,
Besieged by terrors, longing for the dawn!
Whate'er I see or hear, recalls to mind
Some vivid image, recollection sweet;
Sweet in itself, but O how bitter made
By painful sense of present suffering,
By idle longing for the past, though sad,
And by the still recurring thought, "*I was*"!
Yon gallery that looks upon the west;
Those frescoed walls, these painted herds, the sun
Just rising o'er the solitary plain,
My idle hours with thousand pleasures filled,
While busy Fancy, at my side, still spread
Her bright illusions, wheresoe'er I went.
In these old halls, when gleamed the snow without,
And round these ample windows howled the wind,
My sports resounded, and my merry words,
In those bright days, when all the mysteries
And miseries of things an aspect wear,
So full of sweetness; when the ardent youth
Sees in his untried life a world of charms,
And, like an unexperienced lover, dotes
On heavenly beauty, creature of his dreams!

O hopes, illusions of my early days!—
Of you I still must speak, to you return;
For neither flight of time, nor change of thoughts,
Or feelings, can efface you from my mind.
Full well I know that honor and renown

Are phantoms; pleasures but an idle dream;
That life, a useless misery, has not
One solid fruit to show; and though my days
Are empty, wearisome, my mortal state
Obscure and desolate, I clearly see
That Fortune robs me but of little. Yet,
Alas! as often as I dwell on you,
Ye ancient hopes, and youthful fancy's dreams,
And then look at the blank reality,
A life of ennui and of wretchedness;
And think, that of so vast a fund of hope,
Death is, to-day, the only relic left,
I feel oppressed at heart, I feel myself
Of every comfort utterly bereft.
And when the death, that I have long invoked,
Shall be at hand, the end be reached of all
My sufferings; when this vale of tears shall be
To me a stranger, and the future fade,
Fade from sight forever; even then, shall I
Recall you; and your images will make
Me sigh; the thought of having lived in vain,
Will then intrude, with bitterness to taint
The sweetness of that day of destiny.

Nay, in the first tumultuous days of youth,
With all its joys, desires, and sufferings,
I often called on death, and long would sit
By yonder fountain, longing, in its waves
To put an end alike to hope and grief.
And afterwards, by lingering sickness brought
Unto the borders of the grave, I wept
O'er my lost youth, the flower of my days,
So prematurely fading; often, too,
At late hours sitting on my conscious bed,
Composing, by the dim light of the lamp,
I with the silence and the night would moan
O'er my departing soul, and to myself
In languid tones would sing my funeral-song.

Who can remember you without a sigh,
First entrance into manhood, O ye days
Bewitching, inexpressible, when first
On the enchanted mortal smiles the maid,

And all things round in emulation smile;
And envy holds its peace, not yet awake,
Or else in a benignant mood; and when,
—O marvel rare!—the world a helping hand
To him extends, his faults excuses, greets
His entrance into life, with bows and smiles
Acknowledges his claims to its respect?
O fleeting days! How like the lightning's flash,
They vanish! And what mortal can escape
Unhappiness, who has already passed
That golden period, his own *good* time,
That comes, alas, so soon to disappear?

And thou, Nerina, does not every spot
Thy memory recall? And couldst thou e'er
Be absent from my thought? Where art thou gone,
That here I find the memory alone,
Of thee, my sweet one? Thee thy native place
Beholds no more; that window, whence thou oft
Wouldst talk with me, which sadly now reflects
The light of yonder stars, is desolate.
Where art thou, that I can no longer hear
Thy gentle voice, as in those days of old,
When every faintest accent from thy lips
Was wont to turn me pale? Those days have gone.
They *have been*, my sweet love! And thou with them
Hast passed. To others now it is assigned
To journey to and fro upon the earth,
And others dwell amid these fragrant hills.
How quickly thou hast passed! Thy life was like
A dream. While dancing there, joy on thy brow
Resplendent shone, anticipations bright
Shone in thy eyes, the light of youth, when Fate
Extinguished them, and thou didst prostrate lie.
Nerina, in my heart the old love reigns.
If I at times still go unto some feast,
Or social gathering, unto myself
I say: "Nerina, thou no more to feast
Dost go, nor for the ball thyself adorn."
If May returns, when lovers offerings
Of flowers and of songs to maidens bring,
I say: "Nerina mine, to thee spring ne'er
Returns, and love no more its tribute brings."

Each pleasant day, each flowery field that I
Behold, each pleasure that I taste, the thought
Suggest: "Nerina pleasure knows no more,
The face of heaven and earth no more beholds."
Ah, thou hast passed, for whom I ever sigh!
Hast passed; and still the memory of thee
Remains, and with each thought and fancy blends
Each varying emotion of the heart;
And *will* remain, so bitter, yet so sweet!

NIGHT SONG OF A WANDERING SHEPHERD IN ASIA.

What doest thou in heaven, O moon?
Say, silent moon, what doest thou?
Thou risest in the evening; thoughtfully
Thou wanderest o'er the plain,
Then sinkest to thy rest again.
And art thou never satisfied
With going o'er and o'er the selfsame ways?
Art never wearied? Dost thou still
Upon these valleys love to gaze?
How much thy life is like
The shepherd's life, forlorn!
He rises in the early dawn,
He moves his flock along the plain;
The selfsame flocks, and streams, and herbs
He sees again;
Then drops to rest, the day's work o'er;
And hopes for nothing more.
Tell me, O moon, what signifies his life
To him, thy life to thee? Say, whither tend
My weary, short-lived pilgrimage,
Thy course, that knows no end?

And old man, gray, infirm,
Half-clad, and barefoot, he,
Beneath his burden bending wearily,
O'er mountain and o'er vale,
Sharp rocks, and briars, and burning sand,
In wind, and storm, alike in sultry heat
And in the winter's cold,
His constant course doth hold;
On, on, he, panting, goes,
Nor pause, nor rest he knows;
Through rushing torrents, over watery wastes;
He falls, gets up again,
And ever more and more he hastes,
Torn, bleeding, and arrives at last
Where ends the path,
Where all his troubles end;
A vast abyss and horrible,
Where plunging headlong, he forgets them all.

Such scene of suffering, and of strife,
O moon, is this our mortal life.
In travail man is born;
His birth too oft the cause of death,
And with his earliest breath
He pain and torment feels: e'en from the first,
His parents fondly strive
To comfort him in his distress;
And if he lives and grows,
They struggle hard, as best they may,
With pleasant words and deeds to cheer him up,
And seek with kindly care,
To strengthen him his cruel lot to bear.
This is the best that they can do
For the poor child, however fond and true.
But wherefore give him life?
Why bring him up at all,
If *this* be all?
If life is nought but pain and care,
Why, why should we the burden bear?
O spotless moon, such *is*
Our mortal life, indeed;
But thou immortal art,
Nor wilt, perhaps, unto my words give heed.

Yet thou, eternal, lonely wanderer,
Who, thoughtful, lookest on this earthly scene,
Must surely understand
What all our sighs and sufferings mean;
What means this death,
This color from our cheeks that fades,
This passing from the earth, and losing sight
Of every dear, familiar scene.
Well must thou comprehend
The reason of these things; must see
The good the morning and the evening bring:
Thou knowest, thou, what love it is
That brings sweet smiles unto the face of spring;
The meaning of the Summer's glow,
And of the Winter's frost and snow,
And of the silent, endless flight of Time.
A thousand things to thee their secrets yield,
That from the simple shepherd are concealed.

Oft as I gaze at thee,
In silence resting o'er the desert plain,
Which in the distance borders on the sky,
Or following me, as I, by slow degrees,
My flocks before me drive;
And when I gaze upon the stars at night,
In thought I ask myself,
"Why all these torches bright?
What mean these depths of air,
This vast, this silent sky,
This nightly solitude? And what am I?"
Thus to myself I talk; and of this grand,
Magnificent expanse,
And its untold inhabitants,
And all this mighty motion, and this stir
Of things above, and things below,
No rest that ever know,
But as they still revolve, must still return
Unto the place from which they came,—
Of this, alas, I find nor end nor aim!
But thou, immortal, surely knowest all.
This I well know, and feel;
From these eternal rounds,
And from my being frail,
Others, perchance, may pleasure, profit gain;
To *me* life is but pain.

My flock, now resting there, how happy thou,
That knowest not, I think, thy misery!
O how I envy thee!
Not only that from suffering
Thou seemingly art free;
That every trouble, every loss,
Each sudden fear, thou canst so soon forget;
But more because thou sufferest
No weariness of mind.
When in the shade, upon the grass reclined,
Thou seemest happy and content,
And great part of the year by thee
In sweet release from care is spent.
But when *I* sit upon the grass
And in the friendly shade, upon my mind
A weight I feel, a sense of weariness,

That, as I sit, doth still increase
And rob me of all rest and peace.
And yet I wish for nought,
And have, till now, no reason to complain.
What joy, how much I cannot say;
But thou *some* pleasure dost obtain.
My joys are few enough;
But not for that do I lament.
Ah, couldst thou speak, I would inquire:
Tell me, dear flock, the reason why
Each weary breast can rest at ease,
While all things round him seem to please;
And yet, if *I* lie down to rest,
I am by anxious thoughts oppressed?

Perhaps, if I had wings
Above the clouds to fly,
And could the stars all number, one by one,
Or like the lightning leap from rock to rock,
I might be happier, my dear flock,
I might be happier, gentle moon!
Perhaps my thought still wanders from the truth,
When I at others' fortunes look:
Perhaps in every state beneath the sun,
Or high, or low, in cradle or in stall,
The day of birth is fatal to us all.

CALM AFTER STORM.

The storm hath passed;
I hear the birds rejoice; the hen,
Returned into the road again,
Her cheerful notes repeats. The sky serene
Is, in the west, upon the mountain seen:
The country smiles; bright runs the silver stream.
Each heart is cheered; on every side revive
The sounds, the labors of the busy hive.
The workman gazes at the watery sky,
As standing at the door he sings,
His work in hand; the little wife goes forth,
And in her pail the gathered rain-drops brings;
The vendor of his wares, from lane to lane,
Begins his daily cry again.
The sun returns, and with his smile illumes
The villas on the neighboring hills;
Through open terraces and balconies,
The genial light pervades the cheerful rooms;
And, on the highway, from afar are heard
The tinkling of the bells, the creaking wheels
Of waggoner, his journey who resumes.

Cheered is each heart.
Whene'er, as now, doth life appear
A thing so pleasant and so dear?
When, with such love,
Does man unto his books or work return?
Or on himself new tasks impose?
When is he less regardful of his woes?
O pleasure, born of pain!
O idle joy, and vain,
Fruit of the fear just passed, which shook
The wretch who life abhorred, yet dreaded death!
With which each neighbor held his breath,
Silent, and cold, and wan,
Affrighted sore to see
The lightnings, clouds, and winds arrayed,
To do us injury!

O Nature courteous!

These are thy boons to us,
These the delights to mortals given!
Escape from pain, best gift of heaven!
Thou scatterest sorrows with a bounteous hand;
Grief springs spontaneous;
If, by some monstrous growth, miraculous,
Pleasure at times is born of pain,
It is a precious gain!
O human race, unto the gods so dear!
Too happy, in a respite brief
From any grief!
Then only blessed,
When Death releases thee unto thy rest!

THE VILLAGE SATURDAY NIGHT.

The damsel from the field returns,
The sun is sinking in the west;
Her bundle on her head she sets,
And in her hand she bears
A bunch of roses and of violets.
To-morrow is a holiday,
And she, as usual, must them wear
Upon her bodice, in her hair.
The old crone sits among her mates,
Upon the stairs, and spins;
And, looking at the fading light,
Of good old-fashioned times she prates,
When she, too, dressed for holidays,
And with light heart, and limb as light,
Would dance at night
With the companions of her merry days.
The twilight shades around us close,
The sky to deepest blue is turned;
From hills and roofs the shadows fall,
And the new moon her face of silver shows.
And now the cheerful bell
Proclaims the coming festival.
By its familiar voice
How every heart is cheered!
The children all in troops,
Around the little square
Go, leaping here and there,
And make a joyful sound.
Meanwhile the ploughman, whistling, returns
Unto his humble nest,
And thinks with pleasure of his day of rest.

Then, when all other lights are out,
And all is silent round,
The hammer's stroke we hear,
We hear the saw of carpenter,
Who with closed doors his vigil keeps,
Toils o'er his lamp and strives so hard,
His work to finish ere the dawn appear.

The dearest day of all the week
Is this, of hope and joy so full;
To-morrow, sad and dull,
The hours will bring, for each must in his thought
His customary task-work seek.

Thou little, sportive boy,
This blooming age of thine
Is like to-day, so full of joy;
And is the day, indeed,
That must the sabbath of thy life precede.

Enjoy, it, then, my darling child,
Nor speed the flying hours!
I say to thee no more:
Alas, in this sad world of ours,
How far exceeds the holiday,
The day that goes before!

THE RULING THOUGHT.

Most sweet, most powerful,
Controller of my inmost soul;
The terrible, yet precious gift
Of heaven, companion kind
Of all my days of misery,
O thought, that ever dost recur to me;

Of thy mysterious power
Who speaketh not? Who hath not felt
Its subtle influence?
Yet, when one is by feeling deep impelled
Its secret joys and sorrows to unfold,
The theme seems ever new however old.

How isolated is my mind,
Since thou in it hast come to dwell!
As by some magic spell,
My other thoughts have all,
Like lightning, disappeared;
And thou, alone, like some huge tower,
In a deserted plain,
Gigantic, solitary, dost remain.

How worthless quite,
Save but for thee, have in my sight
All earthly things, and life itself become!
How wearisome its days;
And all its works, and all its plays,
A vain pursuit of pleasures vain,
Compared with the felicity,
The heavenly joy, that springs from thee!

As from the naked rocks
Of the rough Apennine,
The weary pilgrim turns his longing eyes
To the bright plain that in the distance lies;
So from the rough and barren intercourse
Of worldly men, to thee I gladly turn,
As to a Paradise, my weary mind,
And sweet refreshment for my senses find.

It seems to me incredible, that I
This dreary world, this wretched life,
So full of folly and of strife,
Without thy aid, could have so long endured;
Nor can I well conceive,
How one's desires *could* cling
To other joys than those which thou dost bring.

Never, since first I knew
By hard experience what life is,
Could fear of death my soul subdue.
To-day, a jest to me appears,
That which the silly world,
Praising at times, yet ever hates and fears,
The last extremity!
If danger comes, I, with undaunted mien,
Its threats encounter with a smile serene.

I always hated coward souls,
And meanness held in scorn.
Now, each unworthy act
At once through all my senses thrills;
Each instance vile of human worthlessness,
My soul with holy anger fills.
This arrogant, this foolish age,
Which feeds itself on empty hopes,
Absorbed in trifles, virtue's enemy,
Which idly clamors for utility,
And has not sense enough to see
How *useless* all life thenceforth must become,
I feel *beneath* me, and its judgments laugh
To scorn. The motley crew,
The foes of every lofty thought,
Who laugh at *thee*, I trample under foot.

To that, which thee inspires,
What passion yieldeth not?
What other, save this one,
Controls our hearts' desires?
Ambition, avarice, disdain, and hate,
The love of power, love of fame,
What are they but an empty name,
Compared with it? And this,

The source, the spring of all,
That sovereign reigns within the breast,
Eternal laws have on our hearts impressed.

Life hath no value, meaning hath,
Save but for thee, our only hope and stay;
The sole excuse for Fate,
That cruelly hath placed us here,
To undergo such useless misery;
For thee alone, the wise man, not the fool,
To life still fondly clings,
Nor calls on death to end his sufferings.

Thy joys to gather, thou sweet thought,
Long years of sorrow I endure,
And bear of weary life the strain;
But not in vain!
And I would still return,
In spite of all my sad experience,
Towards such a goal, my course to recommence;
For through the sands, and through the viper-brood
Of this, our mortal wilderness,
My steps I ne'er so wearily have dragged
To thee, that all the danger and distress
Were not repaid by such pure happiness.

O what a world, what new immensity,
What paradise is that,
To which, so oft, by thy stupendous charm
Impelled, I seem to soar! Where I
Beneath a brighter light am wandering,
And my poor earthly state,
And all life's bitter truths forget!
Such are, I ween, the dreams
Of the Immortals. Ah, what *but* a dream,
Art thou, sweet thought,
The truth, that thus embellished?
A dream, an error manifest!
But of a nature, still divine,
An error brave and strong,
That will with truth the fight prolong,
And oft for truth doth compensate;
Nor leave us e'er, till summoned hence by Fate.

And surely thou, my thought,
Thou sole sustainer of my days,
The cause beloved of sorrows infinite,
In Death alone wilt be extinguished quite;
For by sure signs within my soul I feel
Thy sovereign sway, perpetual.
All other fancies sweet
The aspect of the truth
Hath weakened ever. But whene'er I turn
To gaze again on her, of whom with thee
To speak, is all I live for, ah,
That great delight increases still,
That frenzy fine, the breath of life, to me!

Angelic beauty! Every lovely face,
On which I gaze,
A phantom seems to me,
That vainly strives to copy thee,
Of all the graces that our souls inthral,
Sole fount, divine original!

Since first I thee beheld,
Of what most anxious care of mine,
Hast thou not been the end and aim?
What day has ever passed, what hour,
When I thought not of thee? What dream of mine
Has not been haunted by thy face divine?
Angelic countenance, that we
In dreams, alas, alone may see,
What else on earth, what in the universe,
Do I e'er ask, or hope for, more,
Than those dear eyes forever to behold?
Than thy sweet thought still in my heart to hold?

LOVE AND DEATH.

Children of Fate, in the same breath
Created were they, Love and Death.
Such fair creations ne'er were seen,
Or here below, or in the heaven serene.
The first, the source of happiness,
The fount whence flows the greatest bliss
That in the sea of being e'er is found;
The last each sorrow gently lulls,
Each harsh decree of Fate annuls.
Fair child with beauty crowned,
Sweet to behold, not such
As cowards paint her in their fright,
She in young Love's companionship
Doth often take delight,
As they o'er mortal paths together fly,
Chief comforters of every loyal heart.
Nor ever is the heart more wise
Than when Love smites it, nor defies
More scornfully life's misery,
And for no other lord
Will it all dangers face so readily.
When thou thy aid dost lend,
O Love, is courage born, or it revives;
And wise in deeds the race of man becomes,
And not, as it is prone,
In fruitless thought alone.

And when first in our being's depth
This passion deep is born,
Though happy, we are still forlorn;
A languor strange doth o'er us steal;
A strange desire of death we feel.
I know not why, but such we ever prove
The first effect of true and potent love.
It may be, that this wilderness
Then first appals our sight;
And earth henceforth to us a dreary waste
Appears, without that new, supreme delight,
That in our thought is fondly traced;
And yet our hearts, foreboding, feel the storm
Within, that it may cause, the misery.

We long for rest, we long to flee,
Hoping some friendly haven may be found
Of refuge from the fierce desire,
That raging, roaring, darkens all around.

And when this formidable power
Hath his whole soul possessed,
And raging care will give his heart no rest,
How many times implored
With most intense desire,
Art thou, O Death, by the poor wretch, forlorn!
How oft at eve, how oft at dawn,
His weary frame upon the couch he throws,
Too happy, if he never rose,
In hopeless conflict with his pain,
Nor e'er beheld the bitter light again!
And oft, at sound of funeral bell,
And solemn chant, that guides
Departed souls unto eternal rest,
With sighs most ardent from his inmost breast,
How hath he envied him,
Who with the dead has gone to dwell!
The very humblest of his kind,
The simple, rustic hind, who knows
No charm that knowledge gives;
The lowliest country lass that lives,
Who, at the very thought of death,
Doth feel her hair in horror rise,
Will calmly face its agonies,
Upon the terrors of the tomb will gaze
With fixed, undaunted look,
Will o'er the steel and poison brood,
In meditative mood,
And in her narrow mind,
The kindly charm of dying comprehend:
So much the discipline of Love
Hath unto Death all hearts inclined!
Full often when this inward woe
Such pass has reached as mortal strength
No longer can endure,
The feeble body yields at length,
To its fierce blows, and timely, then,
Benignant Death her friendly power doth show:
Or else Love drives her hapless victims so,

Alike the simple clown,
And tender country lass,
That on themselves their desperate hands they lay,
And so are borne unto the shades below.
The world but laughs at their distress,
Whom heaven with peace and length of days doth bless.
To fervid, happy, restless souls
May fate the one or other still concede,
Sweet sovereigns, friendly to our race,
Whose power, throughout the universe,
Such miracles hath wrought,
As naught resembles, nor can aught,
Save that of Fate itself, exceed.
And thou, whom from my earliest years,
Still honored I invoke,
O lovely Death! the only friend
Of sufferers in this vale of tears,
If I have ever sought
Thy princely state to vindicate
From the affronts of the ungrateful crowd,
Do not delay, incline thy ear
Unto thy weary suppliant here!
These sad eyes close forever to the light,
And let me rest in peace serene,
O thou, of all the ages Queen!
Me surely wilt thou find, whate'er the hour,
When thou thy wings unfoldest to my prayer,
With front erect, the cruel power
Defying still, of Fate;
Nor will I praise, in fulsome mood,
The scourging hand, that with my blood,
The blood of innocence, is stained.
Nor bless it, as the human race
Is wont, through custom old and base:
Each empty hope, with which the world
Itself and children would beguile,
I'll cast aside, each comfort false and vile;
In thee alone my hope I'll place,
Thou welcome minister of grace!
In that sole thought supremely blest,
That day, when my unconscious head
May on thy virgin bosom rest.

TO HIMSELF.

Nor wilt thou rest forever, weary heart.
The last illusion is destroyed,
That I eternal thought. Destroyed!
I feel all hope and all desire depart,
For life and its deceitful joys.
Forever rest! Enough! Thy throbbings cease!
Naught can requite thy miseries;
Nor is earth worthy of thy sighs.
Life is a bitter, weary load,
The world a slough. And now, repose!
Despair no more, but find in Death
The only boon Fate on our race bestows!
Still, Nature, art thou doomed to fall,
The victim scorned of that blind, brutal power
That rules and ruins all.

ASPASIA.

At times thy image to my mind returns,
Aspasia. In the crowded streets it gleams
Upon me, for an instant, as I pass,
In other faces; or in lonely fields,
At noon-tide bright, beneath the silent stars,
With sudden and with startling vividness,
As if awakened by sweet harmony,
The splendid vision rises in my soul.
How worshipped once, ye gods, what a delight
To me, what torture, too! Nor do I e'er
The odor of the flowery fields inhale,
Or perfume of the gardens of the town,
That I recall thee not, as on that day,
When in thy sumptuous rooms, so redolent
Of all the fragrant flowers of the spring,
Arrayed in robe of violet hue, thy form
Angelic I beheld, as it reclined
On dainty cushions languidly, and by
An atmosphere voluptuous surrounded;
When thou, a skilful Syren, didst imprint
Upon thy children's round and rosy lips
Resounding, fervent kisses, stretching forth
Thy neck of snow, and with thy lovely hand,
The little, unsuspecting innocents
Didst to thy hidden, tempting bosom press.
The earth, the heavens transfigured seemed to me,
A ray divine to penetrate my soul.
Then in my side, not unprotected quite,
Deep driven by thy hand, the shaft I bore,
Lamenting sore; and not to be removed,
Till twice the sun his annual round had made.

A ray divine, O lady! to my thought
Thy beauty seemed. A like effect is oft
By beauty caused, and harmony, that seem
The mystery of Elysium to reveal.
The stricken mortal fondly worships, then,
His own ideal, creature of his mind,
Which of his heaven the greater part contains.
Alike in looks, in manners, and in speech,

The real and ideal seem to him,
In his confused and passion-guided soul.
But not the woman, but the dream it is,
That in his fond caresses, he adores.
At last his error finding, and the sad exchange,
He is enraged, and most unjustly, oft,
The woman chides. For rarely does the mind
Of woman to that high ideal rise;
And that which her own beauty oft inspires
In generous lovers, she imagines not,
Nor could she comprehend. Those narrow brows,
Cannot such great conceptions hold. The man,
Deceived, builds false hopes on those lustrous eyes,
And feelings deep, ineffable, nay, more
Than manly, vainly seeks in her, who is
By nature so inferior to man.
For as her limbs more soft and slender are,
So is her mind less capable and strong.

Nor hast thou ever known, Aspasia,
Or couldst thou comprehend the thoughts that once
Thou didst inspire in me. Thou knowest not
What boundless love, what sufferings intense,
What ravings wild, what savage impulses,
Thou didst arouse in me; nor will the time
E'er come when thou could'st understand them. So,
Musicians, too, are often ignorant
Of the effects they with the hand and voice
Produce on him that listens. Dead is *that*
Aspasia, that I so loved, aye, dead
Forever, who was once sole object of
My life; save as a phantom, ever dear,
That comes from time to time, and disappears.
Thou livest still, not only beautiful,
But in thy beauty still surpassing all;
But oh, the flame thou didst enkindle once,
Long since has been extinguished; *thee*, indeed,
I never loved, but that Divinity,
Once living, buried now within my heart.
Her, long time, I adored; and was so pleased
With her celestial beauty, that, although
I from the first thy nature knew full well,
And all thy artful and coquettish ways,

Yet *her* fair eyes beholding still in *thine,*
I followed thee, delighted, while she lived;
Deceived? Ah, no! But by the pleasure led,
Of that sweet likeness, that allured me so,
A long and heavy servitude to bear.

Now boast; thou can'st! Say, that to thee alone
Of all thy sex, my haughty head I bowed,
To thee alone, of my unconquered heart
An offering made. Say, that thou wast the first—
And surely wast the last—that in my eye
A suppliant look beheld, and me before
Thee stand, timid and trembling (how I blush,
In saying it, with anger and with shame),
Of my own self deprived, thy every wish,
Thy every word submissively observing,
At every proud caprice becoming pale,
At every sign of favor brightening,
And changing color at each look of thine.
The charm is over, and, with it, the yoke
Lies broken, scattered on the ground; and I
Rejoice. 'Tis true my days are laden with
Ennui; yet after such long servitude,
And such infatuation, I am glad
My judgment, freedom to resume. For though
A life bereft of love's illusions sweet,
Is like a starless night, in winter's midst,
Yet some revenge, some comfort can I find
For my hard fate, that here upon the grass,
Outstretched in indolence I lie, and gaze
Upon the earth and sea and sky, and smile.

ON AN OLD SEPULCHRAL BAS-RELIEF.

WHERE IS SEEN A YOUNG MAIDEN, DEAD, IN THE ACT OF DEPARTING, TAKING LEAVE OF HER FAMILY.

Where goest thou? Who calls
Thee from my dear ones far away?
Most lovely maiden, say!
Alone, a wanderer, dost thou leave
Thy father's roof so soon?
Wilt thou unto its threshold e'er return?
Wilt thou make glad one day,
Those, who now round thee, weeping, mourn?

Fearless thine eye, and spirited thy act;
And yet thou, too, art sad.
If pleasant or unpleasant be the road,
If gay or gloomy be the new abode,
To which thou journeyest, indeed,
In that grave face, how difficult to read!
Ah, hard to me the problem still hath seemed;
Not hath the world, perhaps, yet understood,
If thou beloved, or hated by the gods,
If happy, or unhappy shouldst be deemed.

Death calls thee; in thy morn of life,
Its latest breath. Unto the nest
Thou leavest, thou wilt ne'er return; wilt ne'er
The faces of thy kindred more behold;
And under ground,
The place to which thou goest will be found;
And for all time will be thy sojourn there.
Happy, perhaps, thou art: but he must sigh
Who, thoughtful, contemplates thy destiny.

Ne'er to have seen the light, e'en at the time,
I think; but, born, e'en at the time,
When regal beauty all her charms displays,
Alike in form and face,
And at her feet the admiring world
Its distant homage pays;
When every hope is in its flower,

Long, long ere dreary winter flash
His baleful gleams against the joyous brow;
Like vapor gathered in the summer cloud,
That melting in the evening sky is seen
To disappear, as if one ne'er had been;
And to exchange the brilliant days to come,
For the dark silence of the tomb;
The intellect, indeed,
May call this, happiness; but still
It may the stoutest breasts with pity fill.

Thou mother, dreaded and deplored
From birth, by all the world that lives,
Nature, ungracious miracle,
That bringest forth and nourishest, to kill,
If death untimely be an evil thing,
Why on these innocent heads
Wilt thou that evil bring?
If good, why, why,
Beyond all other misery,
To him who goes, to him who must remain,
Hast thou such parting crowned with hopeless pain?

Wretched, where'er we look,
Whichever way we turn,
Thy suffering children are!
Thee it hath pleased, that youthful hope
Should ever be by life beguiled;
The current of our years with woes be filled,
And death against all ills the only shield:
And this inevitable seal,
And this immutable decree,
Hast thou assigned to human destiny,
Why, after such a painful race,
Should not the goal, at least,
Present to us a cheerful face?
Why that, which we in constant view,
Must, while we live, forever bear,
Sole comfort in our hour of need,
Thus dress in weeds of woe,
And gird with shadows so,
And make the friendly port to us appear
More frightful than the tempest drear?

If death, indeed, be a calamity,
Which thou intendest for us all,
Whom thou, against our knowledge and our will,
Hast forced to draw this mortal breath,
Then, surely, he who dies,
A lot more enviable hath
Then he who feels his loved one's death.
But, if the truth it be,
As I most firmly think,
That life is the calamity,
And death the boon, alas! who ever *could,*
What yet he *should,*
Desire the dying day of those so dear,
That he may linger here,
Of his best self deprived,
May see across his threshold borne,
The form beloved of her,
With whom so many years he lived,
And say to her farewell,
Without the hope of meeting here again;
And then alone on earth to dwell,
And, looking round, the hours and places all,
Of lost companionship recall?

Ah, Nature! how, how *couldst* thou have the heart,
From the friend's arms the friend to tear,
The brother from the brother part,
The father from the child,
The lover from his love,
And, killing one, the other keep alive?
What dire necessity
Compels such misery
That lover should the loved one e'er survive?
But Nature in her cruel dealings still,
Pays little heed unto our good or ill.

ON THE PORTRAIT OF A BEAUTIFUL WOMAN, CARVED ON HER MONUMENT.

Such *wast* thou: now in earth below,
Dust and a skeleton thou art.
Above thy bones and clay,
Here vainly placed by loving hands,
Sole guardian of memory and woe,
The image of departed beauty stands.
Mute, motionless, it seems with pensive gaze
To watch the flight of the departing days.
That gentle look, that, wheresoe'er it fell,
As now it seems to fall,
Held fast the gazer with its magic spell;
That lip, from which as from some copious urn,
Redundant pleasure seems to overflow;
That neck, on which love once so fondly hung;
That loving hand, whose tender pressure still
The hand it clasped, with trembling joy would thrill;
That bosom, whose transparent loveliness
The color from the gazer's cheek would steal;
All these *have been*; and now remains alone
A wretched heap of bones and clay,
Concealed from sight by this benignant stone.

To this hath Fate reduced
The form, that, when with life it beamed,
To us heaven's liveliest image seemed.
O Nature's endless mystery!
To-day, of grand and lofty thoughts the source,
And feelings not to be described,
Beauty rules all, and seems,
Like some mysterious splendor from on high
Forth-darted to illuminate
This dreary wilderness;
Of superhuman fate,
Of fortunate realms, and golden worlds,
A token, and a hope secure
To give our mortal state;
To-morrow, for some trivial cause,
Loathsome to sight, abominable, base
Becomes, what but a little time before

Wore such an angel face;
And from our minds, in the same breath,
The grand conception it inspired,
Swift vanishes and leaves no trace.
What infinite desires,
What visions grand and high,
In our exalted thought,
With magic power creates, true harmony!
O'er a delicious and mysterious sea,
The exulting spirit glides,
As some bold swimmer sports in Ocean's tides:
But oh, the mischief that is wrought,
If but one accent out of tune
Assaults the ear! Alas, how soon
Our paradise is turned to naught!

O human nature, why is this?
If frail and vile throughout,
If shadow, dust thou art, say, why
Hast thou such fancies, aspirations high?
And yet, if framed for nobler ends,
Alas, why are we doomed
To see our highest motives, truest thoughts,
By such base causes kindled, and consumed?

PALINODIA.

TO THE MARQUIS GINO CAPPONI.

I was mistaken, my dear Gino. Long
And greatly have I erred. I fancied life
A vain and wretched thing, and this, our age,
Now passing, vainest, silliest of all.
Intolerable seemed, and *was*, such talk
Unto the happy race of mortals, if,
Indeed, man ought or could be mortal called.
'Twixt anger and surprise, the lofty creatures laughed
Forth from the fragrant Eden where they dwell;
Neglected, or unfortunate, they called me;
Of joy incapable, or ignorant,
To think my lot the common lot of all,
Mankind, the partner in my misery.
At length, amid the odor of cigars,
The crackling sound of dainty pastry, and
The orders loud for ices and for drinks,
'Midst clinking glasses, and 'midst brandished spoons,
The daily light of the gazettes flashed full
On my dim eyes. I saw and recognized
The public joy, and the felicity
Of human destiny. The lofty state
I saw, and value of all human things;
Our mortal pathway strewed with flowers; I saw
How naught displeasing here below endures.
Nor less I saw the studies and the works
Stupendous, wisdom, virtue, knowledge deep
Of this our age. From far Morocco to
Cathay, and from the Poles unto the Nile,
From Boston unto Goa, on the track
Of flying Fortune, emulously panting,
The empires, kingdoms, dukedoms of the earth
I saw, now clinging to her waving locks,
Now to the end of her encircling boa.
Beholding this, and o'er the ample sheets
Profoundly meditating, I became
Of my sad blunder, and myself, ashamed.

The age of gold the spindles of the Fates,

O Gino, are evolving. Every sheet,
In each variety of speech and type,
The splendid promise to the world proclaims,
From every quarter. Universal love,
And iron roads, and commerce manifold,
Steam, types, and cholera, remotest lands,
Most distant nations will together bind;
Nor need we wonder if the pine or oak
Yield milk and honey, or together dance
Unto the music of the waltz. So much
The force already hath increased, both of
Alembics, and retorts, and of machines,
That vie with heaven in working miracles,
And will increase, in times that are to come:
For, evermore, from better unto best,
Without a pause, as in the past, the race
Of Shem, and Ham, and Japhet will progress.

And yet, on acorns men will never feed,
Unless compelled by hunger; never will
Hard iron lay aside. Full oft, indeed,
They gold and silver will despise, bills of
Exchange preferring. Often, too, the race
Its generous hands with brothers' blood will stain,
With fields of carnage filling Europe, and
The other shore of the Atlantic sea,
The new world, that the old still nourishes,
As often as it sends its rival bands
Of armed adventurers, in eager quest
Of pepper, cinnamon, or other spice,
Or sugar-cane, aught that ministers
Unto the universal thirst for gold.
True worth and virtue, modesty and faith,
And love of justice, in whatever land,
From public business will be still estranged,
Or utterly humiliated and
O'erthrown; condemned by Nature still,
To sink unto the bottom. Insolence
And fraud, with mediocrity combined,
Will to the surface ever rise, and reign.
Authority and strength, howe'er diffused,
However concentrated, will be still
Abused, beneath whatever name concealed,

By him who wields them; this the law by Fate
And nature written first, in adamant:
Nor can a Volta with his lightnings, nor
A Davy cancel it, nor England with
Her vast machinery, nor this our age
With all its floods of Leading Articles.
The good man ever will be sad, the wretch
Will keep perpetual holiday; against
All lofty souls both worlds will still be armed
Conspirators; true honor be assailed
By calumny, and hate, and envy; still
The weak will be the victim of the strong;
The hungry man upon the rich will fawn,
Beneath whatever form of government,
Alike at the Equator and the Poles;
So will it be, while man on earth abides,
And while the sun still lights him on his way.

These signs and tokens of the ages past
Must of necessity their impress leave
Upon our brightly dawning age of gold:
Because society from Nature still
Receives a thousand principles and aims,
Diverse, discordant; which to reconcile,
No wit or power of man hath yet availed,
Since first our race, illustrious, was born;
Nor *will* avail, or treaty or gazette,
In any age, however wise or strong.
But in things more important, how complete,
Ne'er seen, till now, will be our happiness!
More soft, from day to day, our garments will
Become, of woollen or of silk. Their rough
Attire the husbandman and smith will cast
Aside, will swathe in cotton their rough hides,
And with the skins of beavers warm their backs.
More serviceable, more attractive, too,
Will be our carpets and our counterpanes,
Our curtains, sofas, tables, and our chairs;
Our beds, and their attendant furniture,
Will a new grace unto our chambers lend;
And dainty forms of kettles and of pans,
On our dark kitchens will their lustre shed.
From Paris unto Calais, and from there

To London, and from there to Liverpool,
More rapid than imagination can
Conceive, will be the journey, nay the flight;
While underneath the ample bed of Thames,
A highway will be made, immortal work,
That *should* have been completed, years ago.
Far better lighted, and perhaps as safe,
At night, as now they are, will be the lanes
And unfrequented streets of Capitals;
Perhaps, the main streets of the smaller towns.
Such privileges, such a happy lot,
Kind heaven reserves unto the coming race.

How fortunate are they, whom, as I write,
Naked and whimpering, in her arms receives
The midwife! They those longed-for days may hope
To see, when, after careful studies we
Shall know, and every nursling shall imbibe
That knowledge with the milk of the dear nurse,
How many hundred-weight of salt, and how
Much flesh, how many bushels, too, of flour,
His native town in every month consumes;
How many births and deaths in every year
The parish priest inscribes: when by the aid
Of mighty steam, that, every second, prints
Its millions, hill and dale, and ocean's vast
Expanse, e'en as we see a flock of cranes
Aerial, that suddenly the day obscure, will with Gazettes be overrun;
Gazettes, of the great Universe the life
And soul, sole fount of wisdom and of wit,
To this, and unto every coming age!

E'en as a child, who carefully constructs,
Of little sticks and leaves, an edifice,
In form of temple, palace, or of tower;
And, soon as he beholds the work complete,
The impulse feels, the structure to destroy,
Because the self-same sticks and leaves he needs,
To carry out some other enterprise;
So Nature every work of hers, however
It may delight us with its excellence,
No sooner sees unto perfection brought,

Than she proceeds to pull it all to pieces,
For other structures using still the parts.
And vainly seeks the human race, itself
Or others from the cruel sport to save,
The cause of which is hidden from its sight
Forever, though a thousand means it tries,
With skilful hand devising remedies:
For cruel Nature, child invincible,
Our efforts laughs to scorn, and still its own
Caprices carries out, without a pause,
Destroying and creating, for its sport.
And hence, a various, endless family
Of ills incurable and sufferings
Oppresses the frail mortal, doomed to death
Irreparably; hence a hostile force,
Destructive, smites him from within, without,
On every side, perpetual, e'en from
The day of birth, and wearies and exhausts,
Itself untiring, till he drops at last,
By the inhuman mother crushed, and killed.
Those crowning miseries, O gentle friend,
Of this our mortal life, old age and death,
E'en then commencing, when the infant lip
The tender breast doth press, that life instils,
This happy nineteenth century, I think,
Can no more help, than could the ninth, or tenth,
Nor will the coming ages, more than this.
Indeed, if we may be allowed to call
The truth by its right name, no other than
Supremely wretched must each mortal be,
In every age, and under every form
Of government, and walk and mode of life;
By nature hopelessly incurable,
Because a universal law hath so
Decreed, which heaven and earth alike obey.
And yet the lofty spirits of our age
A new discovery have made, almost
Divine; for, though they cannot make
A single person happy on the earth,
The man forgetting, they have gone in quest
Of universal happiness, and this,
Forsooth, have found so easily, that out
Of many wretched individuals,

They can a happy, joyful people make.
And at this miracle, not yet explained
By quarterly reviews, or pamphlets, or
Gazettes, the common herd in wonder smile.

O minds, O wisdom, insight marvellous
Of this our passing age! And what profound
Philosophy, what lessons deep, O Gino,
In matters more sublime and recondite,
This century of thine and mine will teach
To those that follow! With what constancy,
What yesterday it scorned, upon its knees
To-day it worships, and will overthrow
To-morrow, merely to pick up again
The fragments, to the idol thus restored,
To offer incense on the following day!
How estimable, how inspiring, too,
This unanimity of thought, not of
The age alone, but of each passing year!
How carefully should we, when we our thought
With this compare, however different
From that of next year it may be, at least
Appearance of diversity avoid!
What giant strides, compared with those of old,
Our century in wisdom's school has made!

One of thy friends, O worthy Gino, once,
A master poet, nay, of every Art,
And Science, every human faculty,
For past, and present, and for future times,
A learned expositor, remarked to me:
"Of thy own feelings, care to speak no more!
Of them, this manly age makes no account,
In economic problems quite absorbed,
And with an eye for politics alone,
Of what avail, thy own heart to explore?
Seek not within thyself material
For song; but sing the needs of this our age,
And consummation of its ripening hope!"
O memorable words! Whereat I laughed
Like chanticleer, the name of *hope* to hear
Thus strike upon my ear profane, as if
A jest it were, or prattle of a child

Just weaned. But now a different course I take,
Convinced by many shining proofs, that he
Must not resist or contradict the age,
Who seeketh praise or pudding at its hands,
But faithfully and servilely obey;
And so will find a short and easy road
Unto the stars. And I who long to reach
The stars will not, howe'er, select the needs
Of this our age for burden of my song;
For these, increasing constantly, are still
By merchants and by work-shops amply met;
But I will sing of hope, of hope whereof
The gods now grant a pledge so palpable.
The first-fruits of our new felicity
Behold, in the enormous growth of hair,
Upon the lip, upon the cheek, of youth!

O hail, thou salutary sign, first beam
Of light of this our wondrous, rising age!
See, how before thee heaven and earth rejoice,
How sparkle all the damsels' eyes with joy,
How through all banquets and all festivals
The fame of the young bearded heroes flies!
Grow for your country's sake, ye manly youth!
Beneath the shadow of your fleecy locks,
Will Italy increase, and Europe from
The mouths of Tagus to the Hellespont,
And all the world will taste the sweets of peace.
And thou, O tender child, for whom these days
Of gold are yet in store, begin to greet
Thy bearded father with a smile, nor fear
The harmless blackness of his loving face.
Laugh, darling child; for thee are kept the fruits
Of so much dazzling eloquence. Thou shalt
Behold joy reign in cities and in towns,
Old age and youth alike contented dwell,
And undulating beards of two spans long!

THE SETTING OF THE MOON.

As, in the lonely night,
Above the silvered fields and streams
Where zephyr gently blows,
And myriad objects vague,
Illusions, that deceive,
Their distant shadows weave
Amid the silent rills,
The trees, the hedges, villages, and hills;
Arrived at heaven's boundary,
Behind the Apennine or Alp,
Or into the deep bosom of the sea,
The moon descends, the world grows dim;
The shadows disappear, darkness profound
Falls on each hill and vale around,
And night is desolate,
And singing, with his plaintive lay,
The parting gleam of friendly light
The traveller greets, whose radiance bright,
Till now, hath guided him upon his way;

So vanishes, so desolate
Youth leaves our mortal state.
The shadows disappear,
And the illusions dear;
And in the distance fading all, are seen
The hopes on which our suffering natures lean.
Abandoned and forlorn
Our lives remain;
And the bewildered traveller, in vain,
As he its course surveys,
To find the end, or object tries,
Of the long path that still before him lies.
A hopeless darkness o'er him steals;
Himself an alien on the earth he feels.

Too happy, and too gay
Would our hard lot appear
To those who placed us here, if youth,
Whose every joy is born of pain,
Through all our days were suffered to remain;

Too merciful the law,
That sentences each animal to death,
Did not the road that leads to it,
E'er half-completed, unto us appear
Than death itself more sad and drear.
Thou blest invention of the Gods,
And worthy of their intellects divine,
Old age, the last of all our ills,
When our desires still linger on,
Though every ray of hope is gone;
When pleasure's fountains all are dried,
Our pains increasing, every joy denied!

Ye hills, and vales, and fields,
Though in the west hath set the radiant orb
That shed its lustre on the veil of night,
Will not long time remain bereft,
In hopeless darkness left?
Ye soon will see the eastern sky
Grow white again, the dawn arise,
Precursor of the sun,
Who with the splendor of his rays
Will all the scene irradiate,
And with his floods of light
The fields of heaven and earth will inundate.
But mortal life,
When lovely youth has gone,
Is colored with no other light,
And knows no other dawn.
The rest is hopeless wretchedness and gloom;
The journey's end, the dark and silent tomb.

THE GINESTRA,

OR THE FLOWER OF THE WILDERNESS.

Here, on the arid ridge
Of dead Vesuvius,
Exterminator terrible,
That by no other tree or flower is cheered,
Thou scatterest thy lonely leaves around,
O fragrant flower,
With desert wastes content. Thy graceful stems
I in the solitary paths have found,
The city that surround,
That once was mistress of the world;
And of her fallen power,
They seemed with silent eloquence to speak
Unto the thoughtful wanderer.
And now again I see thee on this soil,
Of wretched, world-abandoned spots the friend,
Of ruined fortunes the companion, still.
These fields with barren ashes strown,
And lava, hardened into stone,
Beneath the pilgrim's feet, that hollow sound,
Where by their nests the serpents coiled,
Lie basking in the sun,
And where the conies timidly
To their familiar burrows run,
Were cheerful villages and towns,
With waving fields of golden grain,
And musical with lowing herds;
Were gardens, and were palaces,
That to the leisure of the rich
A grateful shelter gave;
Were famous cities, which the mountain fierce,
Forth-darting torrents from his mouth of flame,
Destroyed, with their inhabitants.
Now all around, one ruin lies,
Where thou dost dwell, O gentle flower,
And, as in pity of another's woe,
A perfume sweet thou dost exhale,
To heaven an offering,
And consolation to the desert bring.

Here let him come, who hath been used
To chant the praises of our mortal state,
And see the care,
That loving Nature of her children takes!
Here may he justly estimate
The power of mortals, whom
The cruel nurse, when least they fear,
With motion light can in a moment crush
In part, and afterwards, when in the mood,
With motion not so light, can suddenly,
And utterly annihilate.
Here, on these blighted coasts,
May he distinctly trace
"The princely progress of the human race!"

Here look, and in a mirror see thyself,
O proud and foolish age!
That turn'st thy back upon the path,
That thought revived
So clearly indicates to all,
And this, thy movement retrograde,
Dost *Progress* call.
Thy foolish prattle all the minds,
Whose cruel fate thee for a father gave,
Besmear with flattery,
Although, among themselves, at times,
They laugh at thee.
But I will not to such low arts descend,
Though envy it would be for me,
The rest to imitate,
And, raving, wilfully,
To make my song more pleasing to thy ears:
But I will sooner far reveal,
As clearly as I can, the deep disdain
That I for thee within my bosom feel;
Although I know, oblivion
Awaits the man who holds his age in scorn:
But this misfortune, which I share with thee,
My laughter only moves.
Thou dream'st of liberty,
And yet thou wouldst anew that thought enslave,
By which alone we are redeemed, in part,
From barbarism; by which alone

True progress is obtained,
And states are guided to a nobler end.
And so the truth of our hard lot,
And of the humble place
Which Nature gave us, pleased thee not;
And like a coward, thou hast turned thy back
Upon the light, which made it evident;
Reviling him who does that light pursue,
And praising him alone
Who, in his folly, or from motives base,
Above the stars exalts the human race.

A man of poor estate, and weak of limb,
But of a generous, truthful soul,
Nor calls, nor deems himself
A Croesus, or a Hercules,
Nor makes himself ridiculous
Before the world with vain pretence
Of vigor or of opulence;
But his infirmities and needs
He lets appear, and without shame,
And speaking frankly, calls each thing
By its right name.
I deem not *him* magnanimous,
But simply, a great fool,
Who, born to perish, reared in suffering,
Proclaims his lot a happy one,
And with offensive pride
His pages fills, exalted destinies
And joys, unknown in heaven, much less
On earth, absurdly promising to those
Who by a wave of angry sea,
Or breath of tainted air,
Or shaking of the earth beneath,
Are ruined, crushed so utterly,
As scarce to be recalled by memory.
But truly noble, wise is *he*,
Who bids his brethren boldly look
Upon our common misery;
Who frankly tells the naked truth,
Acknowledging our frail and wretched state,
And all the ills decreed to us by Fate;
Who shows himself in suffering brave and strong,

Nor adds unto his miseries
Fraternal jealousies and strifes,
The hardest things to bear of all,
Reproaching man with his own grief,
But the true culprit
Who, in our birth, a mother is,
A fierce step-mother in her will.
Her he proclaims the enemy,
And thinking all the human race
Against her armed, as is the case,
E'en from the first, united and arrayed,
All men esteems confederates,
And with true love embraces all,
Prompt and efficient aid bestowing, and
Expecting it, in all the pains
And perils of the common war.
And to resent with arms all injuries,
Or snares and pit-falls for a neighbor lay,
Absurd he deems, as it would be, upon
The field, surrounded by the enemy,
The foe forgetting, bitter war
With one's own friends to wage,
And in the hottest of the fight,
With cruel and misguided sword,
One's fellow soldiers put to flight.
When truths like these are rendered clear,
As once they were, unto the multitude,
And when that fear, which from the first,
All mortals in a social band
Against inhuman Nature joined
Anew shall guided be, in part,
By knowledge true, then social intercourse,
And faith, and hope, and charity
Will a far different foundation have
From that which silly fables give,
By which supported, public truth and good
Must still proceed with an unstable foot,
As all things that in error have their root.
Oft, on these hills, so desolate,
Which by the hardened flood,
That seems in waves to rise,
Are clad in mourning, do I sit at night,
And o'er the dreary plain behold

The stars above in purest azure shine,
And in the ocean mirrored from afar,
And all the world in brilliant sparks arrayed,
Revolving through the vault serene.
And when my eyes I fasten on those lights,
Which seem to them a point,
And yet are so immense,
That earth and sea, with them compared,
Are but a point indeed;
To whom, not only man,
But this our globe, where man is nothing, is
Unknown; and when I farther gaze upon
Those clustered stars, at distance infinite,
That seem to us like mist, to whom
Not only man and earth, but all our stars
At once, so vast in numbers and in bulk,
The golden sun himself included, are
Unknown, or else appear, as they to earth,
A point of nebulous light, what, then,
Dost *thou* unto my thought appear,
O race of men?
Remembering thy wretched state below,
Of which the soil I tread, the token bears;
And, on the other hand,
That thou thyself hast deemed
The Lord and end of all the Universe;
How oft thou hast been pleased
The idle tale to tell,
That to this little grain of sand, obscure,
The name of earth that bears,
The Authors of that Universe
Have, at thy call, descended oft,
And pleasant converse with thy children had;
And how, these foolish dreams reviving, e'en
This age its insults heaps upon the wise,
Although it seems all others to excel
In learning, and in arts polite;
What can I think of thee
Thou wretched race of men?
What thoughts discordant then my heart assail,
In doubt, if scorn or pity should prevail!

As a small apple, falling from a tree

In autumn, by the force
Of its own ripeness, to the ground,
The pleasant homes of a community
Of ants, in the soft clod
With careful labor built,
And all their works, and all the wealth,
Which the industrious citizens
Had in the summer providently stored,
Lays waste, destroys, and in an instant hides;
So, falling from on high,
To heaven forth-darted from
The mountain's groaning womb,
A dark destructive mass
Of ashes, pumice, and of stones,
With boiling streams of lava mixed,
Or, down the mountain's side
Descending, furious, o'er the grass,
A fearful flood
Of melted metals, mixed with burning sand,
Laid waste, destroyed, and in short time concealed
The cities on yon shore, washed by the sea,
Where now the goats
On this side browse, and cities new
Upon the other stand, whose foot-stools are
The buried ones, whose prostrate walls
The lofty mountain tramples under foot.
Nature no more esteems or cares for man,
Than for the ant; and if the race
Is not so oft destroyed,
The reason we may plainly see;
Because the ants more fruitful are than we.
Full eighteen hundred years have passed,
Since, by the force of fire laid waste,
These thriving cities disappeared;
And now, the husbandman,
His vineyards tending, that the arid clod,
With ashes clogged, with difficulty feeds,
Still raises a suspicious eye
Unto that fatal crest,
That, with a fierceness not to be controlled,
Still stands tremendous, threatens still
Destruction to himself, his children, and
Their little property.

And oft upon the roof
Of his small cottage, the poor man
All night lies sleepless, often springing up,
The course to watch of the dread stream of fire
That from the inexhausted womb doth pour
Along the sandy ridge,
Its lurid light reflected in the bay,
From Mergellina unto Capri's shore.
And if he sees it drawing near,
Or in his well
He hears the boiling water gurgle, wakes
His sons, in haste his wife awakes,
And, with such things as they can snatch,
Escaping, sees from far
His little nest, and the small field,
His sole resource against sharp hunger's pangs,
A prey unto the burning flood,
That crackling comes, and with its hardening crust,
Inexorable, covers all.
Unto the light of day returns,
After its long oblivion,
Pompeii, dead, an unearthed skeleton,
Which avarice or piety
Hath from its grave unto the air restored;
And from its forum desolate,
And through the formal rows
Of mutilated colonnades,
The stranger looks upon the distant, severed peaks,
And on the smoking crest,
That threatens still the ruins scattered round.
And in the horror of the secret night,
Along the empty theatres,
The broken temples, shattered houses, where
The bat her young conceals,
Like flitting torch, that smoking sheds
A gloom through the deserted halls
Of palaces, the baleful lava glides,
That through the shadows, distant, glares,
And tinges every object round.
Thus, paying unto man no heed,
Or to the ages that he calls antique,
Or to the generations as they pass,
Nature forever young remains,

Or at a pace so slow proceeds,
She stationary seems.
Empires, meanwhile, decline and fall,
And nations pass away, and languages:
She sees it not, or *will* not see;
And yet man boasts of immortality!

And thou, submissive flower,
That with thy fragrant foliage dost adorn
These desolated plains,
Thou, too, must fall before the cruel power
Of subterranean fire,
Which, to its well-known haunts returning, will
Its fatal border spread
O'er thy soft leaves and branches fine.
And thou wilt bow thy gentle head,
Without a struggle, yielding to thy fate:
But not with vain and abject cowardice,
Wilt thy destroyer supplicate;
Nor wilt, erect with senseless haughtiness,
Look up unto the stars,
Or o'er the wilderness,
Where, not from choice, but Fortune's will,
Thy birthplace thou, and home didst find;
But wiser, far, than man,
And far less weak;
For thou didst ne'er, from Fate, or power of thine,
Immortal life for thy frail children seek.

IMITATION.

Wandering from the parent bough,
Little, trembling leaf,
Whither goest thou?
"From the beech, where I was born,
By the north wind was I torn.
Him I follow in his flight,
Over mountain, over vale,
From the forest to the plain,
Up the hill, and down again.
With him ever on the way:
More than that, I cannot say.
Where I go, must all things go,
Gentle, simple, high and low:
Leaves of laurel, leaves of rose;
Whither, heaven only knows!"

SCHERZO.

When, as a boy, I went
To study in the Muses' school,
One of them came to me, and took
Me by the hand, and all that day,
She through the work-shop led me graciously,
The mysteries of the craft to see.
She guided me
Through every part,
And showed me all
The instruments of art,
And did their uses all rehearse,
In works alike of prose and verse.
I looked, and paused awhile,
Then asked: "O Muse, where is the file?"
"The file is out of order, friend, and we
Now do without it," answered she.
"But, to repair it, then, have you no care?"
"We *should*, indeed, but have no time to spare."

FRAGMENTS.

I.

I round the threshold wandering here,
Vainly the tempest and the rain invoke,
That they may keep my lady prisoner.

And yet the wind was howling in the woods,
The roving thunder bellowing in the clouds,
Before the dawn had risen in the sky.

O ye dear clouds! O heaven! O earth! O trees!
My lady goes! Have mercy, if on earth
Unhappy lovers ever mercy find!

Awake, ye whirlwinds! storm-charged clouds, awake,
O'erwhelm me with your floods, until the sun
To other lands brings back the light of day!

Heaven opens; the wind falls; the grass, the leaves
Are motionless, around; the dazzling sun
In my tear-laden eyes remorseless shines.

II.

The light of day was fading in the west,
The smoke no more from village chimneys curled,
Nor voice of man, nor bark of dog was heard;

When she, obedient to Love's rendezvous,
Had reached the middle of a plain, than which
No other more bewitching could be found.

The moon on every side her lustre shed,
And all in robes of silver light arrayed
The trees with which the place was garlanded.

The rustling boughs were murmuring to the wind,
And, blending with the plaintive nightingale,
A rivulet poured forth its sweet lament.
The sea shone in the distance, and the fields

And groves; and slowly rising, one by one,
The summits of the mountains were revealed.

In quiet shade the sombre valley lay,
While all the little hills around were clothed
With the soft lustre of the dewy moon.

The maiden kept the silent, lonely path,
And gently passing o'er her face, she felt
The motion of the perfume-laden breeze.

If she were happy, it were vain to ask;
The scene delighted her, and the delight
Her heart was promising, was greater still.

How swift your flight, O lovely hours serene!
No other pleasure here below endures,
Or lingers with us long, save hope alone.

The night began to change, and dark became
The face of heaven, that was so beautiful,
And all her pleasure now was turned to fear.

An angry cloud, precursor of the storm,
Behind the mountains rose, and still increased,
Till moon or star no longer could be seen.

She saw it spreading upon every side,
And by degrees ascending through the air,
And now with its black mantle covering all.

The scanty light more faint and faint became;
The wind, meanwhile, was rising in the grove,
That on the farther side the spot enclosed;

And, every moment, was more boisterous;
Till every bird, awaking in its fright,
Amidst the trembling leaves was fluttering.

The cloud, increasing still, unto the coast
Descended, so that one extremity
The mountains touched, the other touched the sea.
And now from out its black and hollow womb,

The pattering rain-drops, falling fast, were heard,
The sound increasing as the cloud drew near.

And round her now the glancing lightning flashed
In fearful mood, and made her shut her eyes;
The ground was black, the air a mass of flame.

Her trembling knees could scarce her weight sustain;
The thunder roared with a continuous sound,
Like torrent, plunging headlong from the cliff.

At times she paused, the dismal scene to view,
In blank dismay; then on she ran again,
Her hair and clothes all streaming in the wind.

The cruel wind beat hard against her breast,
And rushing fiercely, with its angry breath,
The cold drops dashed, remorseless, in her face.

The thunder, like a beast, assaulted her,
With terrible, unintermitting roar;
And more and more the rain and tempest raged.

And from all sides in wild confusion flew
The dust and leaves, the branches and the stones,
With hideous tumult, inconceivable.

Her weary, blinded eyes now covering,
And folding close her clothes against her breast,
She through the storm her fearful path pursued.

But now the lightning glared so in her face,
That, overcome by fright at last, she went
No farther, and her heart within her sank;

And back she turned. And, even as she turned,
The lightning ceased to flash, the air was dark,
The thunder's voice was hushed, the wind stood still,
And all was silent round, and she,—at rest!

THE END.

CPSIA information can be obtained at www.ICGtesting.com
Printed in the USA
LVOW08s1313110816

499990LV00002B/124/P